THE BRIMMING RIVER

RAYMOND FREDERICK BROOKE
The Author

RAYMOND F. BROOKE

THE
BRIMMING
RIVER

ALLEN FIGGIS & CO. LTD. DUBLIN 1961

Made and Printed in the Republic of Ireland
by Alex Thom & Co. Ltd., Dublin.

TO

R.D.B., J.B., B.G.B., G.T.B.

CONTENTS

ILLUSTRATIONS

1. *Headwaters; Circa 1590-1783*

THE time comes, when a man, having travelled a goodly distance downstream the river of life, rests his oars awhile to dwell on things seen and heard along the way. It is natural that his thoughts should then hark back to the headwaters, to the source from which he is sprung, where lies his allegiance, his gratitude.

I, therefore, at the beginning of this book of memories, take leave to describe the line from which I come.

The first of my forebears to arrive in Ireland was Sir Basil Brooke, Knight, who came as a Settler in the reign of Queen Elizabeth the First. As that was nearly four hundred years ago and since my family has lived in Ireland from that time onwards, I think I may claim to be Irish—though I know there are many who would not admit the claim in one of English descent.

[1]It is not known for certain from what immediate branch of the Brooke family Sir Basil came, but there is no doubt that he was a descendant of the Brookes of Leighton as is proved by the fact that he carved their arms as his own on his chimney-piece in Donegal Castle, and they are shown again at the head of the funeral entry in the Heralds Office (now the Genealogical Office), Dublin Castle.

Sir Basil had received large grants of land in Donegal, including the town and Castle of Donegal, which last had been the Castle of the O'Donnells. With the help of Government money he restored the Castle, building in it the Great Hall which still contains his carved stone chimney-piece, with the arms of Brooke of Leighton quartering those of his wife, Anne, daughter of Thomas Leycester, and granddaughter of Rafe Leycester of Toft, near Knutsford in Cheshire, and in the other panel the arms of Brooke of Leighton by themselves. He also built the very fine stone Jacobean Manor house at right angles to the original keep. It is now a well-preserved ruin with the original stone mullions in the windows.

Sir Basil died in 1633, and the following is the funeral entry:—

[2]Sr. Basill Broke of Donigall Knight, deceased the 25th of July 1633. He had to wife Ann d.r of Tho.s Lecester of Toft in Cheshire, by whom he had issue Henry Brooke, and hath to wife Elizabeth daughter of Capt. John Wynter of Durham in Gloucestershire, Ann ma.r to Richard Crofton of Lisoorn in the County of Roscommon, and Elizabeth Brooke un-married, was buried in St. Warboroghs Church in Dublin the 26th of July.

---

[1]All this information on my ancestors in the 16th, 17th and 18th centuries is from research made by my brother, Basil Brooke. He has spent much time on this over a number of years, with considerable success, and I am much indebted to him. (See Appendix A).

[2]Genealogical Office, Dublin Castle. Funeral entries Vo. V. 1622-33.

At the head are the arms of Brooke of Leighton with a crescent for difference, impaling those of Leycester of Toft.

Sir Basil was succeeded by his son Henry. Henry married Elizabeth, daughter of John Wynter of Dyrham, Gloucestershire, who in command of the "Elizabeth" had set out in 1577 with Francis Drake in the "Golden Hind" to sail around the world. They passed the Straits of Magellan where they lost each other in a series of storms and Wynter came back through the Straits alone.

Elizabeth Brooke died about 1638 and her eldest son, Basil, was the ancestor of the elder branch—the Brookes of Donegal.

Henry married, secondly, Elizabeth, daughter of Henry, Lord Docwra of Culmore. She died in 1648 and their line is extinct.

He married a third time in 1652—Anne, daughter of Sir George St.George Knt., M.P. of Carrickdrumruisk, Co. Roscommon, and sister of Sir George St.George who was created a Baronet in 1660. From this marriage descends the younger branch, the Brookes of Colebrooke, of which the Brookes of Summerton are a younger branch again.

In the Rebellion of 1641, Henry Brooke held Donegal Castle and the surrounding district for the King; later when came the Civil War, he, in common with most of the Protestants of English origin, took the side of the Parliament. As a result (and in reward for past services and in settlement of arrears of pay) he was granted most of the Barony of Magherastephanagh, County Fermanagh, forfeited by Lord Maguire for his activities in the Irish Rebellion and the massacres that followed.

It was from this Grant that the Colebrooke Estate of about 30,000 acres was made up.

Sir Henry was knighted in 1664 and died in 1671. By his wishes he was buried in Donegal Abbey beside his first

13

2

wife, Elizabeth Wynter. His widow, Anne, lived until 1686, and was buried in Christ Church Cathedral, Dublin.

Sir Henry's family held on through the difficult times at the end of the seventeenth century and the Great Revolution. They naturally followed the fortunes of the Protestant Succession in the war between William of Orange and James II, and some served afterwards in the War of the Spanish Succession.

Sir Henry had four sons of the third marriage—Thomas, George, Oliver and Richard, and four Brooke grandsons, Henry, George, Theodore and Docwra. Theodore was killed at Guadaloupe. Gustavus Hamilton, afterwards Viscount Boyne, and Colonel Kilner Brazier (sons-in-law of Sir Henry), and his nephew Colonel Richard Crofton, who served in the Siege of Derry, all played distinguished parts.

Thomas Brooke, as the eldest of the St.George marriage, succeeded to the Fermanagh grants. He married Catherine, daughter of Sir John Cole of Newlands, Clondalkin, near Dublin, and from this marriage came the name Colebrooke— given to the house and estate set up by their son Henry before 1718. Thomas Brooke had been an officer in the army of Charles II and of James II, but being a follower of King William was dismissed by Tyrconnell and his name together with that of his half-brother, Basil of Donegal, appears on the Bill of Attainder passed by James II's Parliament. He served in the Regiment raised by his brother-in-law, Lord Drogheda.

After the Revolution, in the more settled times that followed in Ireland, Sir Henry's descendants served in Parliament and as Sheriffs of County Fermanagh. As Governor and Custos Rotulorum of the county they took their place in the public life of the country. They made useful marriages and gradually consolidated the position of their family. Everything improved quietly until the death of Henry (old Sir Henry's grandson) in 1761, leaving two sons, Arthur and

14

Francis. Arthur succeeded to Colebrooke, and married in 1751 Margaret daughter of Thomas Fortescue of Reynolds-town, Co. Louth, and sister of Lord Clermont. They had two daughters—Selina, who married Lord Knapton (after-wards Viscount de Vesci), and Letitia, who married Sir John Parnell, Bt. and so was great-grandmother of Charles Stewart Parnell, M.P., the leader of the Irish Parliamentary Party. Both young ladies were well known for their beauty and charm. Sir Arthur, their father, was a spendthrift—apparently unconscious of the value of money; he was also a gambler on the grand scale. On one never-to-be-forgotten occasion Lady Cathcart came to stay with him at Colebrooke and arrived in a carriage drawn by four magnificent mules. She gambled with her host until he had lost everything in the way of money that, at the moment, he had to lose. He then staked his team of black carriage horses against her mules. She won, and on leaving took with her the mules and the horses, and left Sir Arthur marooned with just the carriage.

He was Sheriff of Fermanagh in 1752 and was created a Baronet in 1764. He was also a Privy Councillor and Custos Rotulorum of the county. It would seem that he took an independent line in politics. The Government manipulators complained that Sir Arthur was ready to accept any favours to be had, but when the time came to produce the help which they expected in return, nothing was forthcoming! In Sir John Blacquiere's "Members of the House of Commons 1770–1773, Notes on Same[1] 1773", the entry under Fermanagh is:—

"Sir Arthur Brooke Bart has the principle int[ts] in the County and will continue to do so while he unites with Archdall. He has the character of being one of the worst tempered men living and very stingy. P.

---

[1]Proceedings of the Royal Irish Academy Volume XLVIII Section C. No. 4. M. Bodkin, S.J.
Notes on the Irish Parliament in 1773, Hodges Figgis & Co., Dublin, 1942.

Mervyn Archdall Esq. Has a very good estate and very good interest in the County.   C."

... The letter "P" denotes "Friend to Government in all reasonable measures", and "C"—"Against all Government measures whatsoever".

A difficult team from Sir John Blacquiere's point of view!

Sir Arthur Brooke's portrait by Hugh Hamilton, in the possession of one of his descendants—Mr. Thomas Vesey Fitzherbert—and a miniature from Summerton, the property of Sir George Brooke, Bt., do not in any way suggest a bad-tempered man. Certainly his successors would have been better pleased if he really *had* been stingy.

There is a tradition that he could have had a peerage, but refused, saying that too many of the peers then being made were unfit for gentlemen to associate with, and that he preferred to remain Sir Arthur Brooke, Baronet. He succeeded his father as Member for Fermanagh and held the seat until 1783, when he became Member for Maryborough until his death in 1785. He scattered his patrimony to the winds. He had inherited through his grandmother's brother, Arthur Cole, Lord Rane-lagh, large and valuable property in the city of Dublin and estates in Dublin, Tipperary and Clare and the estate of West Dean Manor in Wiltshire, in addition to the very valuable settled estate at Colebrooke. At his death there was nothing left except the Colebrooke settled estate, denuded of trees and heavily encumbered. On the credit side he took a keen interest in the development of the linen industry and tried to establish it in his own county and on his own estate. He also kept a pack of hounds which the successors to his estate kept going until well into the 19th century.

In addition to the mortgage, Sir Arthur left another blister —an illegitimate son known as Rafferty. Rafferty grew up to be a postilion at Colebrooke. He was fully aware of his relationship to his employers and knew that they on their side were also aware of the fact. He therefore took and was allowed liberties that an ordinary employee would not have ventured on. However, long after Sir Arthur's death, in the days of his nephew, Sir Henry, Rafferty went a good deal further than could be tolerated and was told that he could no longer remain in Sir Henry's employment. This had happened previously on various occasions, but in a less serious way, and Rafferty had always drifted back to Colebrooke. On this occasion however he gave due thought for a moment, and then said,—"I'll go to the Reverend Thomas. I didn't try *him* yet". The Reverend Thomas was a younger brother of Sir Henry.

2. *Colebrooke; Circa 1783-1800*

SIR Arthur was succeeded in 1785 by his brother, Major
Francis Brooke, of Drogheda's Horse, afterwards The 18th
Light Dragoons. He arrived at Colebrooke with his wife,
Hannah Prittie, sister of the first Lord Dunalley, and a family
of six sons, Henry, Arthur, Francis, Thomas, Richard, and
George Frederick, as well as six daughters—Selina (always
talked of as "Old Aunt Selina" to distinguish her from her
niece of the same name, a daughter of George Frederick),
Maria (afterwards Mrs. Webster), Caroline, (who became
Mrs. Trant), Letitia (Mrs. Howard), Harriet (Mrs. Leeson)
and Elizabeth (Mrs. Carter).

Major Francis immediately set to work to restore the
fortunes of the estate. He and his wife lived very quietly at
Colebrooke cutting down all expenses, doing everything they
could to recoup, and at the same time ploughing money from

their rents back into the estate in improvements such as draining the land and replanting. The following letter preserved among the family papers at Abbeyleix, reveals one of the difficulties facing the Major—the raising of money wherewith to pay off the sums charged on the Colebrooke estate to provide the marriage portions of his nieces, Sir Arthur's daughters—Viscountess de Vesci and Lady Parnell. It is addressed to Lord de Vesci, his niece's husband.

Colebrooke Dec.ʳ 4th, 1786

My dear Lord,

I take this first opportunity of answering your letter as to Mr. Ashe having fourteen thousand pounds to lend at six p. ct.

The estate being only subject to five p. ct. for the portions of Lady de Vesci and Lady Parnell no person who expects six p. ct. will lend his money on knowing this circumstance, without getting collateral security from me, for the extraordinary one per ct. by which I should make myself and personal property after my Decease subject to so much, to the prejudice of my younger children, who are at present very poorly provided for. But perhaps when Mr. Ashe knows how ample the security is and I hope I may add the punctuality with which the interest would be paid he may accept of five p. ct. I don't think he will get six p. ct. for it in England—nor probably here at present, where he will be equally certain as to both security and punctuality in payment of interest. The Estate is subject to legal interest for the four thousand due to Leslie but this sum the widow of Leslie wishes to let lie on the Estate till my convenience to pay it. Therefore the borrowing this last sum from another person, on the same terms, would tend only as to me, to unnecessary expense. However if it would induce a lender to advance Lady de Vesci's and Parnell's portions, to have the entire charge on the Estate together with the circumstance of getting six p. ct. on this last mentioned sum of four thousand, I should waive the consideration of any expense in taking up this last sum also with the other provided it tended to enable me to do what might be agreeable and convenient to you,—as I sincerely wish by every act of mine to merritt and preserve the regard of you Lady de Vesci and family. If the money cannot be had for the interest the Estate is liable to—as long as it is your convenience to let it lie I shall with pleasure during my life pay you six p. ct. for the sum of five thousand pounds from the period of my coming into possession of the Estate.

I have had a thought, if practicable, of getting an act of Parliament to sell the Tip.ʸ estate for the payment of yours and Sr. John Parnell's demand, tho' that estate on the expiration of leases will probably rise treble the present income.

I mean soon to send my son Harry to Cambridge or Oxford, to which tho' there may be objections. I have a great dislike to our College[1] and I think if I don't see with the partiality of a Father he promises well.

Mrs. Brooke and Family join in love to Lady de Vesci and the ladies.

> With my Dear Lord
> Yours truly sincere
> and affectionate
>
> Francis Brooke

---

[1]Trinity College, Dublin.

FRANCIS BROOKE OF COLEBROOKE
Major 18th Light Dragoons, d. 1800.

From this it is apparent that a sum of £10,000 was charged on the Colebrooke Estate for the marriage portions of his two nieces, and in addition £4,000 was owing to Leslie's widow.

There is nothing to show the reason for Major Francis Brooke's dislike of Trinity College, Dublin as a University to which he could send his son Henry. Both Sir Arthur and he himself had graduated there with B.A.—one in 1746, the other in 1755, and Henry's younger brother Thomas was also to enter Trinity in 1792, aged 16.

Before succeeding to Colebrooke Major Brooke with his wife and family had lived at Brookelawn, near Palmerstown, Co. Dublin on the Dublin–Lucan Road. The house is shown on Taylor and Skinner's Road Map and is identified by the words "Brooke Esq.". Brookelawn, still so called, is on the south side of the River Liffey Valley. Frank Brooke's youngest son, George Frederick, was born there in 1779 and eighty-six years later, in 1865, he came to die at Summerton, situated on the high ground on the other side of the Liffey Valley, in sight of his birthplace.

The eldest son, Henry, later created a Baronet, helped and followed his father in the work of restoring the Colebrooke Estate and when he died left a very prosperous property behind him. His eldest son, Francis, was killed at Waterloo. His body was never found. Sir Henry was succeeded by his next son, Arthur, and his property and his Baronetcy went from father to son in direct line down to Victor, Arthur Douglas, and then to the present head of the family—formerly Sir Basil Brooke, B.t—now Viscount Brookeborough, the very able Prime Minister of Northern Ireland. Viscount Alanbrooke is a son of Sir Victor Brooke, and so uncle of the Prime Minister.

Major Frank's next son, Arthur, has the distinction of being, so far, the only member of the family who has found his way into the Dictionary of National Biography. He served in the

44th Foot and commanded the 1st Battalion in Sicily in 1809 and at the capture of Ischia. He also served in Egypt in 1801 and received from the Sultan the gold medal of the Order of the Crescent. In 1814 he was in command of the Battalion in America where it was brigaded with the 4th Foot. Colonel Arthur Brooke was in Command of the Brigade and his brother, Colonel Francis Brooke, C.B. was commanding the 4th Foot. Major General Ross of Bladensburg was in command of the Army and when he was killed at Baltimore, Arthur Brooke succeeded to the Command. A few days before this they had occupied Washington and burnt the Capitol and all the public buildings.[1] Arthur Brooke retired as a Lieutenant General and a K.C.B.

Having retired, he married—late in life—and settled down at Scribblestown, not far from Dublin, where he was much harassed by his small son Arthur, known as Atty. Atty, on one occasion, had disobeyed orders in some way, and being due for correction fled from the attack of his father, retiring in good order into an apple tree. The General followed and sternly called out, "Come down Sir! Come down! and I'll thrash you within an inch of your life!" Atty's response to this attractive invitation was a volley of apples, under which the General was forced to retire. This procedure was repeated until Atty—seeing that his store of ammunition was running out, climbed down from his tree and fled to another when their engagement was re-opened.

A portrait of Sir Arthur, wearing the Sultan's Gold medal and other decorations, painted by Martin Cregan, P.R.H.A. was at Summerton and is now the property of Sir George Brooke.

There were two more soldier sons, Francis and Richard. Francis served, during all his career in the Army, in the 4th The King's Own Regiment of Foot. That Regiment bears

---

[1] Historical record of the 44th Foot. Thomas Carter. Second Edition. Gale & Polden 1887.

on its colours the battle honours of Corunna, Badajoz, Salamanca, Vittoria, San Sebastian, Nive, Peninsula, Bladensburg and Waterloo. And with the exception of Nive and Bladensburg (when he was recovering from wounds) Colonel Brooke was present at every one of these engagements and commanded the Regiment in most of them. He joined in 1791 and retired in 1819.[1] Having served all through the Peninsular War under Sir John Moore and the Duke of Wellington, the Regiment embarked at Parillac on the Garonne on the 29th May 1814 and sailed to America. There, as already stated, the Regiment was brigaded with the 44th under Colonel Arthur Brooke. After the burning of Washington and the death of Major General Ross the 4th were shipped to Port Royal to re-fit and meet reinforcements from England, including Frank Brooke who had been recovering from wounds. They returned to America and took part in a fight at New Orleans where the Colonel was again badly wounded. Almost immediately afterwards, in February 1815, he was nominated Companion of the Order of the Bath. He had already received a Peninsular Gold Medal as well as the Peninsular Gold Cross for Badajoz, Salamanca, Vittoria and San Sebastian. The Regiment returned to Europe and arrived at Ostend on the 12th June 1815, just in time to take part in the Battle of Waterloo. It was formed into a Brigade with the 27th and 40th Regiments, the Brigade commanded by Colonel Brooke, in Major General Lambert's Division.

On the morning of the battle, Colonel Brooke heard a good deal of noise and a voice wailing "[2]Och! Why did I leave my little shop in Killashandra?" He asked what the furore was all about, and was told it was the Regimental Barber who always took on like that on the morning of a fight.

---

[1]Historical record of the Fourth Regiment of Foot. Longman Orme & Co. London 1839.

[2]These anecdotes were collected by Putt, the family butler about 1850–1886, and retailed by him to George Brooke, Frank Brooke's gt. nephew.

In May 1798[1] when the Regiment was at Chatham, it had already received a draft of between three and four hundred Irish youths. It is more than probable that Frank Brooke collected a proportion of these, and as Killashandra in Cavan is not very far from Brookeborough in Fermanagh, the Barber may well have been one of that detachment.

When he left the Regiment in 1819 the officers presented Colonel Frank Brooke with a gold cup.

He married a daughter of George Burdett of the Heath House, Maryborough. As a result of his wounds, the Colonel had not enjoyed very good health and was supposed to live sparingly. His wife limited him to one glass of port but he occasionally insisted on a second, and to meet her unavailing protests he invariably said "My dear this is Salamanca night" (or Vittoria or Badajoz or whatever name came into his head) —"I must drink a toast!" He died in 1826, without issue, and aged about 56. His widow gave his gold cup to his eldest brother, Sir Henry, at Colebrooke; the Peninsula Gold Cross, Waterloo Medal and the badge of the Blew and Orange, (a Society in the King's Own Regt.), to his youngest brother, George Frederick, in the possession of whose great-great-grandson, Sir George Brooke, they now are. His Peninsula Gold Medal was given to his sister, Caroline Trant, whose descendants still have it. The Colonel's widow also gave some of his plate to her own relations.

The last soldier brother was Richard, who served in his father's Regiment, the 18th Light Dragoons. His brother officers used to chaff him, saying that the Regiment had been moved from Windsor because Princess Charlotte had fallen in love with him. (As the Princess was probably twenty years younger than Richard, the story was most unlikely, quite apart from the difference in their social position.) Charles, his only son, served in the 4th Dragoon Guards, the 9th Lancers and in the Osmanli Irregular Cavalry in the Crimean War.

[1]Historical Record. op. cit.

He was a good amateur steeplechase rider and like many another young man in the same position he was chronically hard up, as the following correspondence will show.

November 30th, 1858

3 Victoria Square,

London, S.W.

My dear Uncle,

I am under orders to sail for India on the 11th of December. I understand that Mrs. Leeson's[1] property is to be divided amongst the next of kin, and also hearing that there is a great deal of expense attending the smallest matter of this routine to a person in India I write to know what you think I had better do to make the least trouble and expense being anxious to avoid putting money into the lawyers pockets. Pray my dear Uncle distinctly understand I do not wish to write to you for the purpose of asking for the money before the proper time, but going so far away should like to leave everything connected with business to be arranged in as simple a manner as possible. We should have wished much to have seen you all before going but a pleasure trip to old Ireland is rather beyond me. Letitia is going with me and unites in love to you and the girls also to Francis and his wife. I hope we shall come back laden with rupees and find you all well and with some liver to lend to a friend to enjoy his native country with.

I am, my dear Uncle

Your affectionate nephew

G. F. Brooke Esq.   Chas. C. Brooke.

---

[1]His Aunt, the Hon. Mrs. Robert Leeson, who had recently died, apparently intestate, and whose small Estate was being administered by her brother George Frederick Brooke.

25

The opening sentences of the letter and the reasons for the request are a masterpiece of tactful camouflage, but it is unlikely that his Uncle failed to realise the position. The letter is endorsed:

Dec. 2nd 1858
Chas. C. Brooke,
Ansd. Geo.F.B.
remittance on Bank of England £150 on act. 1st Dividend from Mrs. Leeson's Estate.
Again in August 1859 £100.

The second remittance was sent in response to an appeal sent through Charles's cousin Francis Brooke, George Brooke's son. Charles had not been to India and he would seem to have been a little uncertain as to how his Uncle would receive the request.

Exeter Barracks,
August 4th, 1859

My dear Francis,
The 9th are expected here in a few weeks and the Col. has ordered the Officers to provide themselves with horses without delay. This is of course a great difficulty to me, as you may imagine, therefore if it would not put my Uncle to inconvenience I should very much like to have a part of anything that is likely to come from Mrs. Leeson's Estate as soon as possible but if you think it would annoy him . . . . . "

Evidently Francis kept the rest of the letter as this is all there was of it among his Father's papers.

The final act in the comedy is a receipt!

August 10th, 1859

£100......

> Received from George Frederick Brooke
> Esq.ʳ the sum of one hundred pounds on
> account of the Estate of the late Mrs.
> Leeson.
>
> Chas C. Brooke
>
> 9th Royal Lancers.

It would seem therefore that the old man, who in his day had known what it was to be badly off, did not keep his nephew waiting unduly when there was anything to divide.

Charles eventually settled down as Riding Master at Sandhurst, becoming an almost legendary figure to several generations of Cadets, not least for his colourful language and withering sarcasms.

Major Frank's next son was Thomas. (The Reverend Thomas with whom poor Rafferty hoped to find sanctuary in his distress.) There does not seem to be a great deal known about him, except that he was more of a horse coper than a parson and that he gave his eldest brother Henry a most almighty stick, and for years they were not on speaking terms.

Of the daughters, the eldest—"Old Aunt Selina"—lived in rooms which would probably now be described as "a flat above a shop" in Nassau Street, Dublin. There she received a stream of visitors—mostly elderly beaux from Kildare Street Club just around the corner.

Letitia married Colonel Howard of Castle Howard in County Wicklow; his house, on high ground near Avoca, overlooked the Meeting of the Waters and "Thomas Moore's Tree." Letitia had a long career fairly full of incident. Both she and her husband had hot tempers and the marriage was not a happy one. There were no children. But marriages did

27

not "break up" in those days! Whatever might happen at home, husband and wife in public presented an unbroken front. In due course the Colonel died. Upstairs in her room Mrs. Howard was trying on her widow's weeds, when her man-servant announced that young Doctor McMunn had called. Now this Dr. McMunn had received many kindnesses from the Colonel and was very fond of him. He therefore asked permission of the widow to take a last farewell of his old friend. Mrs. Howard acquiesced and the Doctor was taken to the room where the Colonel was lying. He went close, looked at the body and immediately said—"I don't think he's dead at all! Get me a silver spoon and a glass of Madeira".

These were brought, and the Doctor prised open the Colonel's mouth and poured some Madeira down his throat. The Colonel hiccoughed loudly, coughed a couple of times and tried to sit up. Such is the picturesque description always given of the scene. Whether a doctor would pass it or not I do not know, but the result would be the same. The Colonel recovered and Dr. McMunn acquired considerable merit, and worked up a good practise as a result. In the meantime the disconsolate widow folded up her weeds in tissue paper and put them away. Twelve years later the Colonel died again. This time, though history says nothing definite on the subject, one may accept that the decanter of Madeira was locked up until well after the funeral.

This leaves only George Frederick, the youngest son, and founder of the Summerton branch—the younger one, to which I belong.

facing page 29

GEORGE FREDERICK BROOKE OF SUMMERTON, 1779-1865
(*From the painting by W. Brocas, R.H.A.*)

3.   *The Governor and the Graces; 1779-1865*

MAJOR Frank's youngest son, George Frederick, was born in 1779. He was six years old therefore when his father inherited Colebrooke in 1785 and the move was made from Brookelawn. When he was born his father, noting that all the family Christian names had been used already, decided that they had better call the baby after the Prince of Wales, later George IVth. He was brought up tough at Colebrooke, as bathing arrangements in the house were scanty and primitive. Mrs. Brooke sent her sons out to a pond to bathe and in winter a man accompanied them carrying a pole wherewith to break the ice.

After his father's death in 1800, George Frederick lived in Dublin with his mother. In one of the rebellions he served in the Lawyers' Corps in the Volunteers; his musket was at Summerton together with a pike which he had picked up after a riot in Sackville Street.

He bound himself to a wine merchant in Dublin and set up business on his own account at No. 1 Gardiner's Row in 1806. This action of his gave the family a shock. It was the first breakaway from a family tradition (held in common with many other families of the same kind at that date) that only the Navy, the Army, the Church or the Law were open to younger sons. Commerce was taboo! George held to his views in spite of this opposition and as a result was cold-shouldered by his eldest brother. Henry, however, realising later on how successful his younger brother was, came round and finally requested that he should take George (Sir Henry's son) into the business. He was rather indignant when George Frederick pointed out that he had a son of his own. All the same, Sir Henry stood by his younger brother to the extent that he bought his wine from him.

Being a younger son in a family of twelve, where there was not a great deal of money, George had not sufficient capital. His patrimony was £2,000 and he borrowed their share, £2,000 each from two of his sisters, so that he started with a capital of £6,000, two-thirds borrowed, on which he paid 5%.

He died in 1865, fifty-nine years later, leaving an estate of close on £250,000.

Old George Brooke was always spoken of as "the Governor", and it is by that title that we shall know him from here on. He was tall and held himself erect to the end of his life, and was known among his rivals in the wine trade as the Prince of Merchants. He was a man of character, who was always ready to say what he thought, though he said it in such a way as not to give offence, and he was greatly respected in Dublin. When the Governor was quite an old man, a young customer enquired of him—"Whose claret is this?" . . . meaning to enquire the name of the shipper in Bordeaux from whom it had been bought. To the old man this was quite a new angle of approach, and he replied, "It's mine, Sir, and you may take it or leave it". The young man took the wine but told his friends that Mr. Brooke was a very peppery old gentleman.

On another occasion the Governor received a very large bill of costs from his solicitor. Thinking it excessive, but not being the type to ask for a reduction, he paid up without comment. A few days later as he was making his way along Sackville Street, he met the solicitor in question who took off his hat and said, "It's a fine day, Mr. Brooke". To which Mr. Brooke retorted, "It is, but don't you charge it up in your next bill of costs".

As a young man he was a great friend of the first Lord Norbury, the Chief Justice, who was thirty years older. They used to ride together sometimes in the evening on the north side of Dublin where Lord Norbury lived. At other times— especially during what he called the "kite-flying season", when this pastime (which was apparently indulged in by the children to a very great extent) upset Lord Norbury's mount, they went out to the North Bull at Clontarf. The Governor was very fond of riding, had a good seat and looked well on a horse; however he got little opportunity beyond hacking of the kind described with Lord Norbury. Later on, when he was prospering and could afford to rent a house for the summer in the country (and finally to buy one) he usually rode into Dublin in the morning and home again in the evening. His grandson said that one of the saddest scenes he ever witnessed was the last time the old man came to the stableyard to start for a ride—to find that he could no longer mount or throw his leg over the horse's back. He just turned and walked away without saying a word to anyone. The grandson was on his pony ready to go out with the old man.

The Governor was elected a Director of the Bank of Ireland in 1828 and continued to serve on the Board until 1861[1]. In 1859 the Board was dissatisfied with the Government which was refusing to relieve the Bank from a restriction in

[1] History of the Bank of Ireland, pages 236–238. F. G. Hall, Dublin 1949.

the Charter which prevented it from advancing money on the security of land. The Board, as a preliminary, sent some of its members including George Brooke to interview the Lord Lieutenant, who promised to use his influence with the Government to get the restriction removed. Three members of the Board (one of whom was again George Brooke) were then sent over to London to interview the Chancellor of the Exchequer who finally brought in and passed the required Bill. This was a stout effort on the part of the Governor who was then 80 years of age. Whether travelling by night or day he would have had to sit up in the train all the time. The journey then took between thirteen and fourteen hours, the sea passage being from four and a half to five hours and sometimes more. It was all speeded up in 1860.

The Governor married, in 1814, Jane, daughter of Richard Grace of Boley, Queen's County. She died in 1835. The Graces were a very old family in Kilkenny and Queen's County, being descended from Raymond le Gros who came to Ireland with Strongbow. They owned at one time large tracts known as "Grace's Country" but unluckily for them they chose the unsuccessful side in the seventeenth century struggles and their lands were removed from them piece by piece until in the 18th century, though still fairly prosperous, there was not a great deal left. In 1701 John Grace, the heir, went to London and appealed to his kinsman John Sheffield, Duke of Buckingham, to help him to obtain restoration of part of the family estates. The Duke received him most kindly and made him reside at Buckingham House and all seemed in train towards a successful result. But unfortunately everything crashed when it was discovered that John had seduced the Duke's illegitimate daughter. The Duke "immediately left Buckingham House where Mr. Grace was staying, and retiring to his seat at Richmond, he altogether abandoned him and refused to know any of the family ever after". This unfortunate affair, described by the historian as "an act of moral irregularity and a breach of hospitality"[1], caused the irretrievable loss of something like 33,000 acres of very valuable estates.

Jane Grace had three brothers—William, Sheffield, and Percy. The second brother, Sheffield, was an historian and a genealogist. He made endless research and wrote much valuable history of his family, from which the foregoing facts are drawn.

The youngest brother, Percy, was in the Royal Navy. There is extant a portion of a letter from which the signature is missing and it reads as follows:—

> Ganges, off Bornholm 22nd May
> 1801.

My dear Lord,

I received your letter of the 19th ult. only yesterday, as I had been in the Lynx to Petersburg where Sir Hyde Parker had sent me with dispatches for Count Pahlen, and returned to my ship last night. I am very happy at being able to give you a very favourable and flattering account of your protogee (sic) young Grace who is really the best boy imaginable. A day or so preceding the action of the 2nd he dined with me and in joke I desired the First Lieutenant would station him in the bread Room if we were engaged. He seemed not to take much notice but after two or three minutes the tears flowed from his eyes and I could only make my peace with him by promising he should be with me on the Quarter Deck. As you may imagine he was a little surprised at *first* but he behaved as well as you would wish him and is a most promising lad.

On my way to join the Fleet in Kioga Bay I fell in with the Latona. I changed my quarters from the Lynx and stayed with Lord St.Helens until . . .

---

[1] Memoirs of the Family of Grace by Sheffield Grace, F.S.A., London, 1823.

The letter had the following endorsement on it:—

"This appears to be part of a letter from Captain Thomas Francis Fremantle R.N. Commanding the Ganges, to the Earl Temple, who, with his usual kindness and consideration, forwarded it to my mother.
Percy Grace".

The "action of the 2nd" was the Battle of Copenhagen and Percy Grace was then ten years of age.

He saw much further service and was actively employed all over the world until hostilities ended with the general peace in 1816. Later he was employed for a considerable time on the West Coast of Africa in the suppression of the Slave Trade, having fights with Dutch and French slave traders. He retired as an Admiral. Percy always knocked his biscuits on the table, even in his brother-in-law's house, having formed the habit as a boy when he knocked the ship's biscuits in order to shake the weevils out of them. When his servant brought him small change it always had to be washed in soap and water before being handed to the Admiral on a silver salver.

And this is his cure for Gout—

GOUT POULTICE

1 lb rye meal, 4 ozs. yeast, 2 ozs. salt with a little sweet oil. Made into a thin poultice and applied warm to the part affected. If in the foot to the sole particularly and repeated about every twelve hours or oftener when the poultice becomes dry.
Three or four dressings seldom fail curing a fit of the gout.
Admiral Grace.

Sir William Grace, Jane's eldest brother, is the one whose story has greatly engaged the interest of her descendants. He was, however, a continual source of annoyance to his brother-in-law, the Governor. Sir William scattered his illegitimate children mostly around Dublin, but one as far afield as Italy, and as his whereabouts seemed invariably to have been uncertain, messages and enquiries for him were often left at the Governor's house and office, 1 Gardiner Row. One day, the Governor on returning from the Bank was told by his manservant that a woman had left a parcel for Sir William Grace.

"She just put the parcel in my hands and said, 'That belongs to Sir William Grace'; she gave it to me, and she was off before I could ask her any questions. Will you please come and look at it Sir? I don't like the look of it myself".

"What don't you like about it?"

"I just don't like the look of it, Sir. It moves! Please come and see".

The Governor went to look at the parcel, and sure enough it *did* move, it almost rolled over. They opened the parcel—and found a baby inside with a slip of paper stating that the child belonged to Sir William Grace. The poor little baby was sent off to the Foundling Hospital, and the servant was given orders never to take in another parcel for Sir William Grace.

The illegitimate daughter in Italy lived at Pistoia. This girl was certainly a daughter of Sir William. She was Louisa Grace until she married and became Louisa Grace-Bartolini. Her mother was generally supposed to have been a woman who sold prints in Dublin, but the girl lived in Italy where she passed as the daughter of Sir William's reputed wife. She afterwards married an Italian, Bartolini, who treated her abominably. Sir William had given her money and had settled more on her, prevailing on the much enduring Governor to act as trustee, but Bartolini seized and spent anything that was in his wife's hands. Her mother in Dublin made considerable trouble and invaded the Governor's house when he had to call in the police. These two episodes must have been very trying for a respectable city merchant, who was also a pillar of the church. His name is on the silver alms plates in St. George's Church, as Church Warden when it was built. The money for Louisa was placed on mortgage on land in Ireland, the Governor collecting the interest and sending it on to her. When she died Bartolini applied for the capital but was beaten off.

All his life it was supposed that Sir William was unmarried but after his death a lady appeared—a hitherto unknown female with three small boys and her marriage lines!

For some years the Governor had been in the habit of renting a house in the country on the west side of Dublin, and finally in the 1830's he bought Summerton which he had already rented once or twice. There was about ninety acres of land and a small eighteenth century house to which he added for his own accommodation some reception rooms and bedrooms. Then in 1848 when his son married, he added a "sitting-room" for him and his bride with nursery accommodation over it, which he felt would in due course be necessary. He was correct in his guess and the nursery accommodation was used for sixty years—first for six grandchildren and then for tribes of great-grandchildren.

It was not a very big house nor a very handsome one from the outside, but the rooms were good and comfortable and they were always warm. People often criticise the big old open firegrates, on the grounds that all the heat was wasted by going up the chimney. This is not correct—a certain amount of heat *did* go up the chimney as it was intended to do, but it was not wasted. It remained there keeping the walls warm and dry, an important thing in Ireland where the climate as we were taught by the Governess is "mild but humid".

From the windows and from what was always called by the old-fashioned eighteenth-century name of "the pleasure ground", and from the garden, there were fine views of the Dublin mountains. The place itself was a stretch of land not very wide, running along the top of the "Strawberry Beds" on the North bank of the Liffey and in all directions views of the Dublin mountains could be seen. It was not a large or pretentious house or place, but the recollection of the happiness it produced, of the fun and good talk, the merry cracks and jokes (which eased even the misery of the last day of the holidays)—the few rabbits that were seldom caught but supplied great sport for the beagles; the places where ponies and later horses, could be schooled (not that *I* ever took much part in that if I could possibly avoid it), and finally the love and kindness lavished by their parents in each generation, have given Summerton a warm corner in the affections of those who had the good fortune to be brought up there.

The Governor died on 5th November 1865. He was devoted to his eldest grandson, the second George Frederick Brooke, who was brought back from Eton to see him before he died. Gerald, George's next brother, describing their grandfather's funeral, used to tell him,— "You were up in the first carriage with my father, so you got no real view of the procession as I did, because I was in the last carriage with Putt[1], and as we came through White's Gate[2] he made me hang out of the window so that I could see that the hearse had already passed the Phoenix,[3] and he said, "Now, Master Gerald, that will show you how greatly Mr. Brooke was respected by everyone".

---

[1]Putt, the Governor's butler.

[2]One of the gates of the Phoenix Park.

[3]The Phoenix Monument, erected in the Phoenix Park by the Earl of Chesterfield, about a mile from White's Gate.

4. *Grandmother's Steps*

THE Governor left one son, Francis Richard, my grand-
father, often disrespectfully alluded to by my generation as
"Your Grandfather Francis", and three daughters, Louisa
(Aunt Cobbe) who married Charles Cobbe (Uncle Cobbe)
of Newbridge, Co. Dublin, and Aunts Selina and Georgina.
Uncle Cobbe, who was descended from an eighteenth century
Archbishop of Dublin, had many acres of mixed shooting at
Newbridge and he also owned a grouse moor on the edge of
the Dublin mountains. He used to give his nephews a good
deal of shooting and as they advanced on to the mountain
(he shot over dogs) he was in the habit of saying to them—
"Now boys,—no talking! Remember there is nothing that
ferae naturae dislike so much as vox humana". The boys
were far too blown to talk but the little man never stopped
and suddenly—"Whrrr" ... and a covey of grouse got up

out of shot followed by an agonised cry from Uncle Cobbe—
"God bless my soul, boys. What did I say to you?"

He was also a great retailer of interesting bits of news and
one day he burst in on my grandfather in Dublin (my father,
then a small boy, was in the room) and said, "God bless my soul,
Francis, have you heard? What will Domville do next?"

Domville was Sir Charles Domville of Santry Court—a
very extravagant eccentric with feudal ideas. He was High
Sheriff of County Dublin and had ordained that his tenants
were to follow his barouche, on horseback, from Santry
through Dublin to the Four Courts on the day of the opening
of the Session. My grandfather asked—"What has Domville
been doing now?"

"Well, he has had his procession with his unfortunate
tenants following the carriage. I saw it go by—and two cart
mares foaled in Sackville Street".

Neither of the other two daughters (Selina and Georgina)
married. Jimmie Carroll, who worked at Summerton and of
whom we shall hear more, gave what was said to be a good
impression of them when they were out walking:—

"Miss Georgina walked in front, with Miss Selina a step
behind, and every step they took was a full yard".

Aunt Georgina was the younger but she died first and Aunt
Selina never got over her death and gradually became senile.
However she and her sister had made arrangements some
years before and when she died she left their very considerable
savings to their nephew, my father. As he was just beginning the
very expensive task of educating eight sons this was of great
help and he commented—"If Aunt Selina's head was wrong,
her heart was in the right place".

The Governor's only son, Francis Richard, had married,
in 1848, Henrietta Monck, daughter of Viscount Monck.
Her father was very ill at the time of the marriage so the wedding took place in the drawing-room of his house in Merrion
Square, Dublin—now pulled down to form part of Holles

Street Hospital. The honeymoon was spent at Charleville, his place in County Wicklow, and the bride and bridegroom drove down there after the ceremony. The postilions were in good form, having drunk several toasts, and the horses ran away down Tinehinch Hill—a very steep place with a sharp turn at the bottom—which landed the newly wed couple at Charleville gates, strange to say, in good order.

At the time of the Governor's death, their family was complete, three sons, three daughters; George Frederick, my father, aged 16, Gerald, Johnnie, Louisa, Eva, and Grace, the youngest, aged 2.

My grandfather did not make any great impression. During his father's lifetime he was completely overshadowed and as he only survived him fifteen months, he had no time to make any mark. Then his widow had the extraordinary complex of never talking about any of her dear relations after they were dead, so that there was no chance of getting any information about him from her. She wore mourning all the rest of her life except at family weddings (when she appeared, looking charming, in lavender grey) and she always used black edged notepaper. The only thing my father ever told me about his father was ... "He rode very nicely, but he was no judge of a horse. My Goodness! ... the 'sticks' he used to get".

My grandmother had a sister, Elizabeth, who lived in Paris, and so far as the young were concerned she seems to have been an old trout. The grandparents spent long spells with her in Paris taking with them the two eldest children, George and Louisa (Aunt Loui). As a result these two spoke French well, with a perfect accent, but my father never exhibited this accomplishment in later life. He had never enjoyed the visits to Paris—to him it was all a waste of time that might be better employed riding his pony at home. His father dragged him around the picture galleries, and the astonishing thing is, that in spite of all this he always enjoyed looking at pictures, and later on, was quite a good judge. But as a result he became allergic to foreigners, and one effect the visit to Paris *did* have, was to make him dislike the idea of any tour on the Continent. The only one he ever made was with his cousin, Fitzie Trant; they went up the Rhine and finally reached Vienna from whence they had to come home in a hurry via Hamburg owing to the outbreak of the Franco-Prussian war. Fitzie was queer about tips! He said he saw no object in giving them as they would never see these people again, so my father, who had other views, had to tip for both.

The grandparents often made long visits to Colebrooke, posting the whole way in their own carriage. They had their own horses as far as Clonee, about six miles from Summerton, and from there onwards they posted. Travellers in those days warned the posting establishment in Dublin, shortly before the appointed day, of the destination, the date on which they wished to go, together with details of the hour and route. Fresh horses were then waiting, with postboys, along the way at the regular changing places. Each stage was about ten miles. It was advisable to tip the postboy well at the end of each stage, as he warned the boy taking over of any shortcomings and the fresh boy behaved accordingly. My grandparents usually started from Summerton soon after an early breakfast and if all went well they reached Colebrooke in plenty of time for dinner that evening. In those days that meal took place a good deal earlier than became the fashion later on. The distance was about 110 miles and time was lost changing horses—so they made good going.

My father was at Eton when the Governor died and apparently his father had been in correspondence with his Tutor, "Johnnie Yonge" on the subject of the next brother, Gerald, going there too. A letter on the subject runs:—

Eton, Oct. 25th 1865.

My dear Sir,

George did not suffer from his journey I hope, but he had more of a cold on him when he started, than I liked and he promised to be careful.

With regard to preparing his brother for Eton, it is desirable that he should be as well *grounded* as possible in Latin and Greek parsing. He should know the *Latin Grammar* and the *Greek Accidence* with its rules. He should practise *Latin exercises* either in simple short sentences or longer connected passages, if he is forward enough, and *Latin verses*.

The choice of books is not very material, if he has passed the Delectus, he cannot do amiss with Virgil for Latin and Xenophon for Greek.

He should read some Ancient History. He will be examined also in Arithmetic; proportioned to his age and general acquirements.

With our united kind remembrances, Believe me

My dear Sir

Very faithfully yours

John Eyre Yonge.

and then,

August 2nd 1866

Eton College

Windsor.

My dear Sir,

I hope your sons had a pleasant journey yesterday evening and reached you when expected. George does pretty well in his lessons, and shows fair regularity and attention to them, but he requires much to put him on a fair level with his place in the School, and I hope he will take pains to keep up and master what he has done.

He ought to go over again what he has recently done in at least one Greek and one Latin book, and add to it some Ancient History, which he is defective in the knowledge of.

His brother is very backward, and was of course thrown back by his illness. I see he has got his remove but he is the last.

It will be very desirable for him to have some lessons regularly, if possible, in Latin and Greek Grammar and verses. He is a very good boy like his brother. I have no faults to find. I was sorry to miss seeing them off. I forgot they were going so soon. Their holidays are to last until Friday Sept. 28.

> Believe me,
> My dear Sir,
> Very faithfully yours,
> John Eyre Yonge.

School reports go in double harness with the laws of the Medes and Persians. Thirty-five years later the pattern had not changed. No matter how well you did you ought to have done better:—

"Could do better, if he would try. He must concentrate".

Gerald left Eton after his father's death to go to a crammer. Having committed some frightful atrocity he was sacked but made such an eloquent appeal for the "orphan and his widowed mother" that he was reprieved.

My grandfather only outlived his father by 15 months, but he put off making a will until it was too late for him to think it out, and have it properly drawn up by the family lawyer. He therefore left complications behind him which caused trouble right to the end. He had been told quite unexpectedly that he was fatally ill with only a short time to live, and proceeded without the help of the lawyer to make a will. He left Summerton to my grandmother (who from here on will be called Grannie) for her life with the power of appointment to whichever of the three sons she chose—ignoring the fact that the Governor had settled it all on my father. My father who was then about 18 was amazed when he was told of this arrangement, and said that he could not understand it, as his grandfather had always told him that Summerton was to be his. No one seems to have taken the trouble to look at the old man's will so Grannie reigned at Summerton for some thirty years, quite unconscious of the fact that she should have handed it all over to her son on his 21st birthday. When he married, he had to set up at Pickering in County Kildare, spending a great deal of money on that house; his younger brothers and sisters lived with his mother in his house at Summerton, sometimes to effect economy (having overspent their incomes), while my father weighed in with cheques.

Finally, being the only son left, Grannie asked him to come and live with her at Summerton, and then the situation became so impossible that at the urgent request of my mother she was told the real position by her eldest daughter, Mrs. Hamilton. She then handed over, much aggrieved at having been allowed to remain for so long in a false position. I fancy my father had known for some time but had said nothing as he wished to spare his mother. Then when things became impossible he consented to her being told.

Grannie had one failing which is quite a common one with Irish people—the postponing of necessary repairs until it is almost too late. My father always said that she would never send her brougham to the coach builder to be looked over until the whole carriage was just held together by the varnish, and then it had to be almost rebuilt, repainted all over and varnished, at considerable expense. The same thing happened at Summerton, and when my father took over, the repairs to the roof of the house and in the stableyard almost amounted

JOHN KANE
The Bagpipe Man

to rebuilding. The truth was that her jointure was not sufficient to meet what she had undertaken under her husband's
will and though my father helped her from time to time with
substantial cheques, he was still faced with the bills for repairs
at the end.

Most country houses in Ireland had a following of people
who came at intervals to receive sustenance. Summerton
was no exception and Grannie had quite a large clientele.
These people were not "beggars" in the ordinary sense of
the word. They never whined or asked for money—they
just arrived and took up a position knowing that if they did
not come too often they would receive some help. Most of
them had some compensation to offer. Some entertained the
establishment with music, some who travelled over a wide
country (often taking in several counties) were accepted because
of the news they brought of friends and relations who lived
many miles away. They brought news of what was going on;
whether good sport was being had with the hounds, what
the fishing on the lakes had been like—or again they just
carried idle gossip. Others were good conversationalists,
worth entertaining, and they were all naturally weather-
wise. Most of them did not work and probably had never
done any work. They may have been of the type described
by Synge "in a family of peasants, where the average comfort
is just over penury, the gifted son sinks . . . and is soon a
tramp on the roadside". Indeed they might almost be described
as the Oliver Goldsmiths of a lower stratum of society.

My grandmother's sitting-room had a window just above
ground level which looked out on the same side of the house as
the Hall-door. The more privileged members of her clientele
were allowed to tap on the window to give notice of their
arrival. She opened the window to greet them. There was
always a window-box with a thick growth of plants in it so
that they could not see into the room. Grannie had a short
conversation which varied in length according to the particular

45

category into which the visitor fitted, then she gave him his pecuniary dole and sent him around to the back door.

Others of a lower grade sat on the hall-door steps until she came out for her morning walk. They did not ring the bell as that meant bringing someone to the door who might be offended at having been brought from work downstairs to attend to them, though as a rule the callers were on good terms with everybody. The ritual was much the same as that prescribed for the more privileged section—a little conversation, two or three coppers and then round to the back door. One and all received the same treatment—a small bowl of soup if it was a lucky day and always some bread and cold meat sandwiches. It was accepted as bad form to eat the food at the door, so it was stowed away in some sort of receptacle which they had about their persons and eaten at a suitable sheltered place somewhere along the road.

Of these visitors pride of place must go to Kane "the Bagpipe Man". He was known over a very wide tract of country, generally travelling as far as Athlone, but I do not think he ever crossed the Shannon. Kane was an albino, his sight was very bad and about him there was a peculiar, slight, but not repellent, scent of beeswax which I suppose he used to rub on his pipes. These were different from the pipes usually seen nowadays, as the player could not walk and play at the same time. Kane stood on his left leg, the right leg being rested on the crook of his walking-stick which he placed under his thigh not much above the knee. He had a piece of old cloth which he put on the stick to form a pad. The support of the pipes was then stood up on his leg. He did no blowing with his mouth and the wind was supplied by a bellows strapped against his right arm which he worked to and fro against his ribs. From inside the house you heard a noise like a swarm of bees and then a blast of music announced that Kane had arrived and was off on one of his pieces. Of course this was an enormous treat for everybody, and very popular. Kane was rewarded by many others in the house as well as by Grannie.

Then there was "Shaky", whose real name was George MacCormack. He was always neatly turned out—wearing a hat, a man's shooting cape which someone had given him, and carrying a heavy walking stick. He had a pied-à-terre at Mullingar, and he also travelled as far as Athlone, but again not beyond the Shannon, covering quite a large tract of Westmeath, Longford and Meath. He was a special ally of Grannie's youngest daughter, Grace (Mrs. Malone). Aunt Grace in due course had a small clientele of her own. Once after a very severe blizzard, while the snow was still lying deep, a tinker came to the door of her house looking for help. He said he and his wife and "young babby" were sheltering under a rough tent in the back of a ditch. He received the usual bread and meat and some milk for the baby, and went on his way. Aunt Grace turned to her butler who had been a witness of the scene and said, "Lennon, did you see? That unfortunate man, out in the blizzard, had nothing on under his coat". Lennon replied in a voice that was almost a wink . . . "Maybe, Ma'am, he was dressed for the o-casion".

Incidentally it was always well to take a kindly attitude when dealing with a tinker. In a town in the Midlands a woman was brought up before the Magistrates at Petty Sessions. The young Royal Irish Constabulary Constable who was prosecuting, informed the Bench, "Your Worships, the defendant belongs to the she-tinker class. I found her at 2 a.m. this morning walking up and down the village street, calling upon all and sundry to come out and fight her. She was under the influence of drink. So I arrested her, your Worships, and I took her to the station, where I charged her in the correct legal manner. With that, your Worships, she flung herself down on the broad of her back. She drew all her petticoats over her head and assumed a most threatening demeanour".

47

Another character of the old days was "Bulge Pocket"—
so-called from the enormous pockets into which he stuffed
food and anything else he could get. He was known by no
other name and being invariably filthy was looked on rather
with disfavour.

And there was yet another itinerant, this one slightly
eccentric in that he called himself "Lord John D. Vienne
(de Vienne)" as if he was some sort of Austrian nobleman.
He was a special friend of my cousin Dick Brooke, who with
his brother and sister lived with Grannie. "Lord John" was
in fact very fond of Dick as the following correspondence
with Grannie will show. (It will be seen by the dates that
this was long after she left Summerton, showing that her
clientele had followed her to the house she had rented, Mount
Hybla, near Castleknock. The change was very acceptable
as it gave the characters another port of call.) Dick was
serving with Mounted Infantry in South Africa when the
letter reached his Grandmother:—

Johnstown Navan
4.5.1900.

To the Honourable Mrs. Brooke

    I am very anxious to know how Master Richard is
I hope he getting on well.

Yours faithfully
Lord John

Grannie sent her reply to "Lord John" (that being the only
name she knew for him) at the address given on his letter,
and received the following some time later:—

Avenue Hotel
Belfast

9 Aug 1900

Sir John F. Dillon presents his compliments to the
Honble. Mrs. Brooke and returns her letter in the
envelope in which it was sent to him.

... The writer was Sir John F. Dillon of Lismullen near Navan to whom the Post Office people at Navan had sent the letter, as being the only "John" with a title that they knew of in the neighbourhood.

My grandmother also had another letter:—

Duleek
July 11, 1900

To the Hon. Mrs. Brooke

Dear Madam,

Just a few lines to inquire if you have heard anything lately from Mr. Richard he being a great friend to me. I sincerely hope he is in the enjoyment of good health also your Ladyship and all the family. Your Ladyship will excuse me for tormenting you by writing so often but the person who wrote the last letter to you for me omitted putting the right address inside in consequence of which your letter to me was I believe returned.

You will please write and let me know how Mr. Richard is as I am working with Capt. Nicholason it may be sometime before I see any person who can tell me news of him.

I remain Hon. Madam
Your humble servant
    Thomas Boylan
       alias Lord John
           Care John Heade Duleek Co. Meath
The Hon. Mrs. Brooke.

The date—July—in "Lord John's" second letter may be a slip for August but in either case it is a first class example of how the Irish bush telegraph worked. This letter was the first intimation of "Lord John's" real name.

When Grannie settled at Mount Hybla she added a recruit to her collection. The gate opened on to the road but there was no Lodge. She had her cows in the field through which her avenue passed and so the gate always had to be kept shut. Grannie found it a considerable trial if she was alone to have to get out of her carriage to open and shut the gate, but opposite the gate on the other side of the road there was a heap of stones used for road repairs and on this heap there was always sitting a man with a red beard, wearing a decayed frock coat. He was said to be slightly "touched" and he walked out from Dublin every day to his heap of stones, and back again in the evening.

Grannie made a bargain with him—that for half a crown a week he would open the gate when required to do so and shut it again. She never found out that he restricted this office to her own personal service and flatly refused to open the gate for anyone else! On one occasion at Easter he came to her for his usual weekly payment and as an Easter offering she gave him a second half-crown. At the end of the next week when paying him, she graciously asked, "Well, Brady, what did you do with the half-crown I gave you last week?" Brady grinned from ear to ear and said "I got awfully drunk".

In the early days when Grannie took over Summerton after her husband's death, she was greatly helped by Doctor Maguire who doctored all the neighbourhood and so knew the history and character of almost everyone. He had in addition been a Regimental Surgeon in the Army and was therefore an expert at sorting out the malingerers from the genuine cases. He acted as Grannie's almoner, and when anyone arrived about whom she knew nothing she would send him or her to Doctor Maguire for a report. As they for the most part could neither read nor write, the correspondence was usually open. On more than one occasion he sent her a piece of paper on which was written—"Have nothing whatever to do with the bearer; a most disreputable woman".

Again, the doctor was seeing someone at Summerton when a new client arrived. He had only one arm and said he had lost the other in the Crimea, and was in a pitiable condition. Grannie asked Dr. Maguire to have a word with him and accordingly the doctor went out to have a look.

He began, "My poor man, so you lost your arm in the War"—then without warning he made a sudden spring and tore open the man's coat and shirt, triumphantly bringing forth the arm as a conjuror brings the rabbit out of the hat.

When Grannie talked about dead people or a death in the family or worse, she put on what was known as the dead face and employed a special sepulchral voice. When her nephew died she put on the face and laid on the voice and said to her enthralled descendants "Your cousin Stanley married a Lady we didn't quite care about." Stanley had a brother who at the time of the disaster, put the matter more crudely. He burst in on my Father and shouted, "George! The most awful thing has happened, Stanley's gone and married a whore."

My mother inherited all the old stagers at Summerton and one was added—a celebrity called Miss Fox. She was a very handsome old woman and although referred to as *Miss* Fox, it was well-known that she had two grown-up daughters in Chapelizod, where she lived. It chanced that there was an unfortunate occurrence at Summerton about this time, when a housemaid, quite unexpectedly, had a baby. A few days after the event I was in the room that had been Grannie's sittingroom, with the window open, when Miss Fox sailed past and met Kynes the butler. She said, "I was sorry, Mr. Kynes, to hear of the trouble you had in the house." Whereupon Kynes replied brightly, "Well, Miss Fox, boys will be be boys and girls will be girls, all the world over".

"Ah! you may say that, Mr. Kynes, but I was young meself once, and begob if a man'd flather me, he'd blow the head o'me".

Grannie had a proper opinion of what was due to herself

as Mrs. Brooke. Out one morning for her usual walk around the garden and pleasure ground, she met Jimmie Carroll who was very drunk. She immediately said, "Carroll, leave the garden—by the gate". The last direction was superfluous as he was much too drunk to get out any other way. Unfortunately Carroll chose to retort—"Though you were the Queen of England, I'd black your face".

Now the fact of his being drunk was not a serious misdemeanour. He would go home and sleep it off and to-morrow could return to work—a bad headache being considered sufficient punishment for his foolishness and no more would be heard of the matter. But the enormity of the threat in the reply on this occasion was lèse-majesté of the worst description, and Carroll was sacked there and then.

He did not come back to work at Summerton until well on in my father's time and he was employed from then until his death—partly as a pension. Carroll's job was to keep tidy a walk that ran the whole length of the place overlooking the Liffey, to keep the shrubs pruned and to see that the bushes near the wall did not obscure the views. He was never hustled, and considering his age and infirmities, it was surprising how much work he did. Being very stooped and suffering from rheumatism, he had a donkey which he used as a crutch, to help him up the hill from his house near the river to Summerton. He placed one arm over the donkey's back and had his stick in the other hand and so, half supported, half towed, he made his way to work every day. Having held conversation with him we formed the opinion that it was a great pity that he had remained absent from Summerton for so many years. He had quite a fund of knowledge of the kind found in old books on the properties of shrubs and plants, and also of the treatment of shrubs; he was very self-opinionated and did not care about being given instructions. My mother one day said to him, diffidently, that she thought he was pruning a certain shrub at the wrong time of year. Carroll quite firmly disagreed with her. Then, greatly daring, she ventured, "But, Sir Frederick Moore[1] told me that what I say is correct".

Carroll said, "Is it Moore of the Botanics? Ha! there's nothin' Moore knows that *I* don't know, but there's things *I* know that Moore doesn't know".

He was so stooped that he had to turn up his face to you when he spoke, and he kept one eye tight shut and twisted his mouth at the end of the remark as if he was imparting confidential information of the highest importance. He told us that Purge (Spurge) Laurel was of great efficacy as a medicine.

"You boil the leaves in wather, cutting off the stalk and little bud at the butt, and if you drink the wather, it'll make you vomit, but if you chew the stalk and the little bud, saving your presence, it'll purge you".

He had a lot of information about old times, as he had been employed by the Governor and even before that time had worked as a boy for the people from whom the Governor bought the place. He talked of my grandfather who at that time had been dead for forty years, as "Mr. Francis".

My Uncle Gerald's two sons, Richard and Ralph, known to us as Dick and Gougs, and his daughter, Clementina, called Clemency, lived at Summerton with their grandmother. They were almost uncontrolled and they led her Steward, Fitzsimons, who was not much good anyway, the life of a dog.

Carroll told us that he discovered Fitzsimons "and wasn't he going to attack Master Richard and Master Ralph and Miss Clementina with a hay fork, an' I stood into him and I says to him . . . 'Look at here Fitzsimons, says I, I've known them childer and their da, and their grand-da, and their great-grand-da, man and boy for forty years, and if you so much as harm one hair of their heads, I'll bruise you into the

---

[1]Sir Frederick Moore, Curator of the Botanical Gardens, Glasnevin, a horti-
culturist with a world-wide reputation.

sole of your boots'. Wid that Fitzsimons walked away. But wasn't he the bad man. Wasn't he cot after, above in Fetherstonhaughs, milking the cows in the field".

Carroll's wife, who died before him, was the poetess of the district. I have been told by a critic whose opinion I respect, that she took some of her ideas and lines from Tennyson; I doubt very much however if she had ever read any of his poetry. On the other hand, there is the possibility that Tennyson drew on Mrs. Carroll . . . .

Only two poems survive . . . "Keatings were disgraceful people", and "A Short Description of the Strawberry Beds". "Keatings" is the earlier of the two, and is addressed to her son. It is supposed to describe how the Carrolls set up in the small cottage in which they lived (and eventually died), the difficulties they had over the arrears of rent which they had to pay before Keatings would, or perhaps could, surrender the house. There is mention of the appalling condition of the cottage, the help Mrs. Carroll received, and finally how Carroll by his own hard work turned it into a comfortable home:—

KEATINGS WERE DISGRACEFUL PEOPLE.

I might not come here at all,
But not to let the cabin fall,
Keatings could no longer live,
Or get any one to give
Them five pounds pay two years' rent,
Which we did before they went.

And when we got it
Top and bottom it was rotted,
Without as much roofing dry
As I could put the bed to lie.

And every wet night would require
To get up and light the fire,
And keep throwing out the door
Cans of water off the floor.

I had to call on many a friend
Who kindly did me money lend.
Miss Armstrong, my constant friend,
Did every three months money send.
When her allowance always came
I had my portion of the same.

I made her dresses, bonnets, caps,
And all her other little traps.
She thought no one like me could seam,
And paid me like a little queen.

We worked our best with heart and hand
For to improve this little spot of land,
To have a quiet little home
For ourselves and our only son.

The only thing gave me concern
Was parting him his trade to learn.
God gave him goodness and success,
And I have reason since to bless.

And every time when work was slack
Your Da he always did come back.
To help the place he would attack
He carried stones on his back
Across the river in a sack.

To make the place a little neat
He built the garden wall and gate,

Put in the steps and made the mound,
And cleared the landings you see around.

The room he also did secure,
Where there was none he made a floor.
He built the chimney, bought a grate,
To have a fire where he could ate
His meals along with you and Kate.

There is one thing I could desire,
If your Da could make it a little higher,
And from the window could look out
And see the lovely dotted trout
In the river swiftly rise
Above the water catching flies.

But there is another thing in keep:
He would have a room for you to sleep,
If Lord Annaly he would ask
Kindly to assist the task;
He is willing, I am told,
To help his tenants with his gold,
To make their little homes secure.

A SHORT DESCRIPTION OF THE STRAWBERRY BEDS.

Mount Sackville Convent is at the head,
Where young ladies they are bred,
And taught by Nuns of every form
The duties woman's life adorn.

Beside it Mr. Guinness built a tower:
It has a clock strikes every hour.
It can be heard from far and near,
And gives the working people cheer.
It lets them know their time to quit,
They may go home to eat their bit.

Near to that is a seat of knowledge,
At Castleknock Saint Vincent's College,
Where the Clergy train up youth,
And teaches them the love of truth,
And every virtue they require,
For the Lord detests a liar:
Even when the truth they tell
You can't believe them very well.

Turning round to your right
Mr. Murphy's castle all in white,
And from his pleasure ground
Can see the country all around.

Next, Mr. Gibney at the Hill,
You will never find him standing still;
He is always making some improvement.
He gives employment to the poor—
He never sends them from his door.

All along sweet Anna river,
Where the playful fishes quiver,
And the anglers patient stand
To try and hook them to the land.

Mrs. Williams keeps the Strawberry Hall.
Never pass without a call.

She is a kindly cheerful woman,
And will be glad to see you coming.
Her place was lately renovated,
And you will be highly accommodated.

Next at woody corner you may stand
And take a view around the land.
Carroll's cottage it is there,
With flowers around to make it fair.
He is a moulder by his trade,
And can show you castings he has made.

It's at the end of Somerton Road
That leads to Lady Brooke's abode.
You will see her gates of wide expansion
Leading to her most lovely mansion,
Where a family of the rarest
Of noble sons and daughters fairest,
A loving mother they surround—
The greatest blessing to be found.
And now, lovely grandchildren quite a score,
If I could name them many more.
And from their terrace wall can view
All that pass the valley through.

Mr. Ennis keeps the Wren's Nest,
A little farther than the rest,
And has charming shady bowers
Where you might spend some happy hours.

There's also some lovely hills.
But sad to see are idle mills
Falling down beside the waters,
And our willing sons and daughters
To another country sped
For to try and earn their bread.

The "Strawberry Beds" is the name given to the steep slopes on the north side of the Liffey Valley. For many years they were intensively cultivated as market gardens which produced a great deal of the early potatoes, vegetables and more especially the strawberries for the Dublin market. Then the speeding up and improvement of transport enabled the Channel Islanders to get their produce in earlier, and gradually the cultivation of the strawberries ceased. The strawberries were a species and were known locally as the "Strawberry Beds strawberry". They were rather pale in colour and of bad shape and would not stand up for a moment in the market at the present day beside the shapely scarlet berries now sold, for the customer looks for something that catches the eye, rather than its plain sister that pleases the palate. They were very sweet, these old strawberries, and of first-class flavour, and excellent for making jam. Most of the private gardens in the neighbourhood had a bed of them cultivated for that purpose. It was the fashion to drive out from Dublin for strawberries-and-cream and to bring back baskets of fresh strawberries and other produce.

The "Mr. Guinness" (mentioned in the poem) is Mr. Edward Guinness, afterwards Sir Edward Guinness, and then Lord Iveagh. This name for him gives a clue to the date of the poem as he was created a baronet in 1885; so it would have been written somewhat earlier than that.

"The Tower" is a building in the style of a Venetian campanile, and was built to supply water to the Guinness house at Farmleigh. The water was pumped up from the Liffey near the mills known locally as "New Holland". They were so called because of a tradition that the Duke of Ormonde established linen mills there, partly to encourage manufacturers in Ireland and partly to aid the artizans who were coming into Ireland as a result of religious persecution on the Continent.

"Saint Vincent's College", was a comparatively small

school at the time when Mrs. Carroll was writing. It has since been tremendously enlarged and its imposing buildings and large playing fields can be seen from the surrounding roads. The college is not really close to the "Strawberry beds"; it is further away from the river near the ruins of the old Castle of the Tyrrells.

"Mr. Murphy's Castle all in white" is still there, with its magnificent views up and down the valley and across to the Dublin mountains.

"Mr. Gibney" owned the Public House called the "Angler's Rest" on Knockmaroon Hill.

"The Strawberry Hall" is on the road which runs through the Liffey Valley at not much above the level of the river. This road is called the "Lower Road" to distinguish it from the other road to Lucan which runs through Chapelizod and Palmerston.

The "Moulder" was Carroll's son, not Carroll himself.

"Lady Brooke" was Grannie—a courtesy title conferred on her by Mrs. Carroll.

"The Terrace Walk" is the walk which it was Carroll's job to tend at the end of his days.

"The Wren's Nest" tavern is still there—a charming early building still kept by a descendant of Mr. Ennis.

"The Idle Mills" are the ruins of a large Mill, complete with Miller's House, known in the locality as "The Devil's Mill". The legend is that Colonel Henry Luttrell of Luttrells-town Castle who owned a great deal of property in the neighbourhood, wished to have a fine mill built for himself on the Liffey. He is reputed to have made a compact with the Devil, by which the latter undertook to build the mill in one night—in return for Luttrell's soul, when the time came. The Devil fulfilled his part of the contract but by some means Luttrell was able to outwit him and so avoided having to keep his side of the bargain.

Henry Luttrell was murdered in Stafford Street in Dublin,

FRANCIS RICHARD BROOKE, 1817 to 1867
(*From the painting by W. Brocas, R.H.A.*)

whilst sitting in a hackney chair, in October 1717. His son, Simon, was created Baron Irnham, and later Earl of Carhampton, and his grand-daughter, the Hon. Mrs. Anne Horton, by marrying in 1771 the Duke of Cumberland, brother of George III, became the immediate cause for the introduction of the Royal Marriage Act.

Her brother, Colonel Luttrell, afterwards 2nd Earl of Carhampton, opposed Wilkes in the Middlesex Election in 1769 and so figures in Junius' letters. Her sister, Elizabeth, who played high and cheated at cards, went abroad and was convicted of picking pockets at Augsberg. She was sentenced to sweep the streets chained to a wheelbarrow, and not long afterwards committed suicide.

Near the Devil's Mills, just below the weir, there is quite a nice Salmon Pool. I read recently an account of this Pool in which it was described as "free". It was not free in the ordinary sense of the word, as it belonged to my father. He owned a fee farm grant which covered, at a small rent per acre, quite a large area all round the neighbourhood and in addition to the rents there went with it the rights of Hunting and Hawking, Shooting and Fishing. This meant that the fishing on the left bank of the Liffey for about a mile from the corner of Luttrellstown wall to a place called the Arches, under Brooke-lawn, belonged to him. I asked him once why he did not take steps to preserve it for himself and he said it was so short a stretch of the river that it was not worth while employing a bailiff, that none of us fished and finally . . . "The people who fish it are local people, almost all employed by me, and if they get some fun out of it I am not going to stand in their way".

All the same it *did* belong to him. He owned it until his death when it passed to my brother Francis and it was taken from him in one of the Land Transactions passed in the Dail since the Treaty.

61

Returning to the subject of Grannie—after she had gone to live at Mount Hybla there were further adventures with a drunken gardener named Phelan.

I suppose as he grew good vegetables—and plenty of them—for the house, she thought his convivial habits did not much matter. Aunt Grace came back from the garden one day and asked what the fearful roaring was that she had just heard. Grannie said, "That must be Phelan. Grace dear, would you mind going out to the garden, and just look in and tell me if he has hung his trousers on the gooseberry bushes. He always does that when he's drunk and of course then I don't go into the garden".

Grannie lived on until 1911 when she was 81, enjoying all her faculties right to the end.

Dick Brooke, the eldest of the cousins who lived with Grannie, was a most delightful character. His stories of people at home and abroad never failed to amuse for he had the gift of slight exaggeration that goes for so much in the make-up of the born raconteur.

One of his sagas was an account of the visit of a small party of the real haute noblesse who came to tea with himself and his brother and sister. Grannie and the mother of the visitors came up to the nursery to see how the children were faring, and were just in time for the end of a drama. Dick and Co. had a Nannie who was known as "Nana Close"; when the ladies arrived she had firm hold of Dick and was saying to the nursery-maid,

" 'Ere Eliza, 'old Dickie tight while I prise Clementina off the little Lady" . . . then (pointing to another guest) . . . "I think Gougie's killed that one".

There was a neighbour called Larry Warren, a small farmer and market gardener and in addition a cattle dealer on a large scale. Dick often held long converse with him and one day, while they were talking, Larry suddenly roared at a small boy who with the help of a gun was frightening rooks off the strawberries. When the boy reached them Larry shouted at him, "Look at here, young fella, if ever I catch you loadin' that gun wid stones agin, I'll cut yer breeches to ribbons on your rump", and then turning to Dick he said quietly, "Isn't that all fair and square, Master Richard".

My father had let two large and valuable fields to Larry who, when the time came to surrender them, refused to do so, claiming that they came under the Land Acts and that he had tenant's rights. They went to law, Larry lost the case, and relations as a result were rather strained. Dick's explanation for this (derived from Larry) was that "he had refused to lend Diver (an appalling mongrel collie) to run wid yer Uncle's dogs". The "dogs" were a very smart pack of dwarf foxhounds, of Belvoir and Brocklesby blood, used as harriers and bred by my father, of which he was justly proud.[1]

Dick, who was known as Michael in his Regiment—the Oxford and Bucks Light Infantry, was killed in Mesopotamia during Townshend's advance to Kut.

[1] See Appendix B.

5. "Mrs. B."

ON my grandfather's death the position at Summerton became somewhat uncertain. After a year my father went up to Cambridge, still worried about his father's will and in the dark as to why he was not the owner of Summerton as he had been assured by the Governor would be the case.

Outwardly it does not seem to have worried him very much and he gradually accepted the situation, but when he came of age he was the eldest son, owning the landed estate, though the rents from it were charged with his mother's jointure, and a fair amount of the expenses of Summerton fell on him. There was quite a lot of entertaining and he acted as host to the friends and relations who came to stay, and at dinner parties and all the usual country house amusements. He did not care for games, but his younger brothers were fond of cricket and there were matches for them in the summer.

Among those who played was their cousin, Charles Stewart Parnell[1]. They never liked him as he always had a grievance of some sort and was inclined to be sulky. He spoiled the enjoyment of the parties and so he was gradually allowed to drop out.

This had nothing of course to do with politics, as it all took place some years before Parnell started on his public career. He was three years older than my father.

My father's real amusement was hunting and riding generally. He was a first-class judge of a horse, a fine horseman and he went well to hounds. In 1872 he won the first "Kildare Red Coat Steeplechase" riding his own horse "Shiner" and in the following year his mare "Lady Rose", ridden by Reggie Greville (known as "The Limb") won the corresponding race in Meath, my father being ill at the time. The riders and owners in these races had to be members of the Hunt and wearing full hunting kit, hence the name. These races afterwards developed into the modern Point-to-Points.

My father only stayed at Cambridge for a year, at the end of which time he told his trustees that if the idea was to further his education, he was only wasting his time and his money! He does not seem to have gone racing but hunted a good deal and always said afterwards what a joy it was to return to the good grass fields of Kildare and Meath.

Back to Dublin he came, to start in the Governor's wine business, which had been left equally between his two brothers and himself, and in 1871 he spent the weeks of the Bordeaux vintage with the Bartons at Chateau Langoa. One of the interesting sidelights he noticed there was that M. Daniel Guestier (the French partner in the firm of Barton and Guestier, and acknowledged to be the finest judge of Claret in Bordeaux), used to throw away his cigar just before he went in to taste, thereby showing that a smoker can also be

[1] Great grandson of Letitia Brooke, Lady Parnell, and leader of the Irish Parliamentary Party.

a first class judge of wine. It has to be admitted that neither my father nor his brothers took the day-to-day interest that they ought to have done in their wine business, which was still bringing them in good incomes.

He also hunted in Cheshire, while he was courting his cousin, Annie Shakerley, whom he married in 1875. It then became necessary for him to find somewhere to live and he bought Pickering, near Celbridge, in County Kildare. He had to spend a good deal of money enlarging the existing house and building all the usual domestic offices. In the meantime, he continued to live at Summerton, where his wife died in June 1877, giving birth to their son, George. Pickering was then left empty.

George grew up, went to Eton in due course, and then served in the South African war in the Hampshire Militia. He received a commission in the Irish Guards when the Regiment was raised, and retired after some years. He went back to the Regiment in 1914 at the outbreak of War. He was sent out to France almost immediately, and died on 5th October 1914 of wounds received the previous day near the Aisne.

My father lived on at Summerton until 1881 when he married my mother, Emily Alma Barton. They had known each other slightly for some time and became engaged at a fancy dress ball given by Mr. & Mrs. Edward Guinness[1] at their house in St. Stephen's Green. My mother's dress was a copy of that worn by Ellen Terry as *Olivia* in the play of that name, adapted by W. G. Wills from Goldsmith's "Vicar of Wakefield" and my father was dressed as Michael Hardey, as depicted in the frontispiece by John Leech in Surtees' "Handley Cross", but adapted for evening wear.

They immediately started to get Pickering into order and went to live there after the wedding in April 1881.

*   *   *   *

[1]Afterwards Sir Edward and Lady Guinness, and then Lord and Lady Iveagh.

"MRS. B."

My maternal grandmother, who was born on 2nd January 1827, was Emily Martin, daughter of James Martin of Ross, County Galway. *Her* mother had been Anne Higinbotham most of whose relations came from or lived in the North of Ireland. My great-grandmother had possessed some money —an important consideration in a wife in the West of Ireland (but not as much as James Martin had hoped for); her father had been swindled out of a fairly large fortune, whereupon he committed suicide. Anne died at the birth of a fifth daughter and the five small children were left to be brought up at Ross by their widowed father, James Martin, who thought them an encumbrance, and his unmarried sister Marian, who treated them very kindly. Marian, so far as she herself was concerned, had odd views on diet. If she ate anything that disagreed with her, she took the earliest opportunity of eating some more of it on the grounds that she refused to be dictated to by her stomach. This strongminded attitude agreed with her, as she lived to be a very old woman.

Mrs. James Martin (Anne Higinbotham) had a younger sister, Jane, who was married to another Martin—the Rev. James Martin—no relation whatsoever to the Martins of Ross. The Rev. James was the Rector of Inver, near Larne in County Antrim, and Emily and her elder sister Mary went to stay with their Uncle and Aunt at Inver Rectory in the winter of 1842. Emily was then in her 16th year.

Emily Martin was undoubtedly lovely, as every one who remembered her in her younger days has remarked, and as her pictures bear witness, though of them the criticism always was that they did but scant justice to her looks. During that visit to Inver Rectory the Barklies gave a dinner-party at Inver House, which developed into an informal dance in the drawing-room, the carpet being left on the floor. The two girls—Emily and Mary—did not dine, but came in afterwards for the dancing. While they were sitting alone in the drawing-room waiting for the diners to come in, two young men, James

67

McCalmont and Hugh McCalmont Cairns (afterwards Earl Cairns, Lord Chancellor of England) walked into the room. James McCalmont glanced at Emily Martin and made some remark to Cairns, which the girls did not catch, but which seemed to amuse him. As soon as possible, James McCalmont had himself introduced and of course Emily Martin danced with him. She said afterwards she might have given him two more dances, but she could not remember.

The following afternoon, Mrs. Martin took her nieces for a drive in her carriage to Park Hill, Carrickfergus, this being the fashionable occupation of the day for ladies of the neighbourhood. As they were driving along at a stately pace, they were passed by a very smart phaeton driven by a young man who took off his hat to Mrs. Martin. Emily asked her aunt who he was and was told—"That's James McCalmont driving back to Abbeylands after the dance".

The following day, the Rector at Inver was sent into a flutter on receiving a letter from James McCalmont—in which he said that he wished to propose for the hand of Miss Emily Martin! Miss Emily Martin was highly amused at the idea, and treated the whole affair as a great joke, saying that it must be a mistake as she would not know the man again if she saw him. Her uncle and aunt however were appalled at the levity with which the proposal was received. James McCalmont was regarded by everyone as one of the most eligible bachelors in the North of Ireland, whilst Emily Martin was one of five sisters whose mother was dead, and whose father's one idea was to get them married off and out of the way, so that he could marry again and beget a son and heir.

After considerable anxious discussion, Mrs. Jane Martin wrote to James Martin telling him of the proposal and of the way it was being received. Martin came at once from Galway to Inver, threatened and abused his daughter in no measured terms, and ordered her to accept James McCalmont's offer. She finally consented to do so. She was then taken back to

Ross to await her wedding—and there complications set in.

There was living at the time at St. Cleran's, Co. Galway, one, James Hardiman Burke (who had married an O'Hara, a cousin of the Martins)—and about him a curious story was told. During the year that he was High Sheriff of Galway a man had been tried for his life and condemned to be executed. As Sheriff, it was Burke's job to provide an executioner, and to see that the sentence was duly carried out. By some mischance he failed to secure a hangman and accordingly had to carry out the sentence himself. Riding home from the gaol that day, he passed an old woman sitting at the side of the road, rocking to and fro, and wildly keening. He stopped to ask if he could help. The old woman, looking up, recognised him and cried out that she was the mother of the man Burke had just executed. *She then proceeded to curse him!* She said that he had killed *her* son—and might none of *his* ever die in their beds.

Burke had three sons, the eldest John, eventually died, unmarried; the second, Robert, perished in the bush in Australia while acting in command of the Burke and Wills exploratory expedition; the other, James, was killed in the Crimea.

John Burke, the eldest son, who was in the Buffs, met and fell in love with Emily Martin, and persuaded her to elope with him. All arrangements were made, as to date and meeting-place, and a message was to be sent at the last moment to Emily telling her the exact hour at which she was to meet Burke. John sent the message by an old servant who somehow found out what it was all about, and, who, fearing the wrath that would fall on his head afterwards, took it to John Burke's mother. She immediately told the Martins what was hatching.

James Martin flew into a towering rage with his daughter who, being completely cut off from John Burke, had to face the storm alone. Being possessed of considerable spirit she retaliated by saying that whatever might happen, nothing would now induce her to marry James McCalmont. Her father said he would soon bring her to reason, and following the practice of the day, locked her up in her room where she was fed on bread and water. He visited her from time to time, but as he only stormed at her she showed herself more and more determined not to give in. The siege went on for some time, James Martin still raging, and Emily still determined not to give in.

Finally, her grandfather, Robert Martin, said that if his son would leave the girl alone and allow *him* to talk with her, something might be done. Emily Martin was very fond of her grandfather, and to the end of her life often talked of him, quoted his sayings and related his doings—while on the other hand she never mentioned her father. Robert Martin therefore went to see Emily and after talking quietly for some time asked if for his sake she would consent to marry James McCalmont. She still said "No!"—but less firmly and her grandfather persisted—"For *my* sake? Surely you wouldn't break an old man's heart?" Finally Emily gave in—but on one condition, that she should be allowed to see James McCalmont alone and tell him the whole story herself; if after hearing it he still wished to marry her, then she would go through with the wedding. The interview took place. After hearing the story, James McCalmont insisted that he still wanted to marry her, and for her own sake he urged her to consent, saying that he would do what he could to make her happy. He pointed out what she indeed well knew, that if she remained at Ross after what had happened she had a fairly miserable time ahead of her.

So the engagement was on again, and the wedding was fixed for 27th April 1843—Emily Martin's age being then sixteen years and four months.

Two days before the wedding, she had a quarrel with her sister Mary, starting with words and ending up in a real fight. In the middle of the set-to the two sisters had each other by the hair, when their Aunt Marian came into the room.

She separated the belligerents and proceeded to lecture them on such behaviour—finally turning to Emily, saying . . . "And you! To think that you should behave like this, when in two days' time you'll be a married woman with an establishment of your own".

To which Emily retorted . . . "Well, you know perfectly well I don't want to marry. I'm only doing it to please all of you".

The wedding took place as planned and after a final interview with her grandfather in which he told her he hoped she would not act too literally on the words of the psalmist— "Forget also thine own people and thy father's house", the bride and bridegroom started off—the bride literally howling. When they arrived at the gate of Ross there was a large gathering of tenants and so forth, and the new Mrs. McCalmont insisted on having the carriage stopped while she shook hands with each one of them.

The first house they put up at on their wedding tour was the Robert McCalmonts' house in Eaton Square, London. It was more formal than anything that Emily McCalmont had been accustomed to, and after the happy-go-lucky over-crowded establishment at Ross it appeared so gloomy that she and the maid she had brought with her, when they went to her room, sat down together on top of her trunk and wept, wishing they were home again in County Galway. The bridal pair then went on to stay with another brother-in-law, the Rev. Thomas McCalmont, near Southampton. His son, Blundell, about eleven years of age was more a contemporary of the bride than anyone else in the house. She romped with him, ran races and finally jumped hurdles, which so scandal-ised the rest of the family that after a consultation, they deputed the Rev. Thomas to talk to her and explain how extremely unbecoming such behaviour was on the part of a young married woman. However things finally settled down and then it occurred to Mrs. McCalmont to ask her husband what it was he had said to young Cairns on first seeing the two girls in the drawing-room at Inver.

He said . . . "I told him that I intended to marry you".

Old Robert Martin might well be thought to have put unfair pressure on his granddaughter, but probably he knew more about his son's character than the rest of the family and realised that the only chance of happiness for Emily would lie in the hands of James McCalmont whom he trusted, and who would take her right away from Galway and all its surroundings. If that was his plan, he was completely justified by the result.

James Martin was a wretched creature. Later on he treated her younger sister Elizabeth in such a way that Emily and her second husband (Augustine Barton) broke off all relations and refused to have anything more to do with him.

James McCalmont must have been a man of fine character as well as great personal charm. The marriage in spite of its extraordinary start, was a complete success during the six years it lasted. Then James died, quite unexpectedly, leaving his widow with two small sons—Hugh[1] and Jimmie[2].

Mrs. McCalmont was an inveterate hero worshipper, and the Duke of Wellington was the hero of her youth. Her mother's uncle, Conway Benning, a Captain in the 66th Foot, had been killed at Albuera. He was a very good looking, attractive young man but unfortunately when he went away to join the Army in the Peninsula, he left behind him (near Ballycastle in Co. Antrim) a farmer's daughter who was shortly to have a baby. Benning had given her the only things he possessed —a charming miniature of himself, and his very large and handsome gold watch. The girl cut out a piece of paper which exactly fitted inside the cover of the watch, and on it she pricked with a pin:—

"For Love and Conway Benning".

---

[1] Major General Sir Hugh McCalmont, K.C.B.

[2] James M. McCalmont, for many years M.P. for North Antrim.

Later on, when he received it from the Duke of York, Commander-in-Chief, the young man's father, Archdeacon Benning, sent the girl the Gold Medal for the Battle of Albuera.

Mrs. McCalmont (Emily) was on one occasion at a ball where the Duke of Wellington was present, and someone asked her if there was anything that would add to her enjoyment of the evening; she, recollecting Conway Benning's romance and his death at Albuera, asked if it would be possible for her to be presented to the Duke. This was arranged and he shook hands with her and was very charming. For years she kept the glove she had been wearing at the time—and then unfortunately lost it. Her eldest son, Hugh, said that perhaps it was as well she had been wearing gloves, as she might have taken it into her head never to wash the hand again!

Years later when she was Mrs. Augustine Barton, and again a widow, acting for her son Sir Hugh McCalmont, she was able to buy up all the relics of Conway Benning.

After James McCalmont's death she took a house in Dublin and with her two small sons divided her time between it and her mother-in-law's home, Abbeylands, in Co. Antrim. In time she met and married Augustine Barton whose home at Rochestown, near Cahir, in Co. Tipperary, was an attractive house placed on high ground overlooking the River Suir. It had come to his mother from an uncle, Colonel Lawford Miles, and Augustine Barton was brought up there, accustomed to living the life of a well-to-do country gentleman. He was born in 1814 and had two brothers, one older, one younger. Unfortunately when about twenty-four, Augustine had developed a weak chest and was threatened with consumption.

He was sent abroad, on sea voyages, and spent some winters at various places on the Mediterranean coast. Then he went off to Australia where he spent some years, and his health apparently improved. The gold rush was on at the time, and by some means, though both his father and mother were alive, he succeeded in securing his portion (as a younger son) of

£10,000. He invested all this in real estate, and continually wrote home to his father and elder brother imploring them to send him out money which he could put out at ten, twelve and even more per cent "and safe as the Bank of England".

Unfortunately a squeeze came, money was required for calls, Augustine had kept nothing back to meet such a situation —so everything went! He always said that at one time he owned all the land on which Melbourne was afterwards built, but he could not hold on, and told my mother and her sister Rose,—

"If everything had gone right with me, you two would be the richest heiresses in Ireland to-day".

However that might have been, he came home across Canada, and when he got to Ireland, his possessions consisted of a case of Australian butterflies, a piece of gold quartz in a crystal locket which he wore on his watch-chain (and which now belongs to me) and the full outfit of a Red Indian Brave. This last he acquired in Canada, and wearing it at a fancy dress ball in Dublin he completely captivated Mrs. James McCalmont who consented to become Mrs. Augustine Barton. He did not come to her quite unendowed as his mother had died not long before and had left him her very nice house in Fitzwilliam Square, Dublin, completely and well furnished. Here his wife was able to entertain to her heart's content— and further, he had been called to the Bar, and from that (in the way things could be done in those days) secured quite a lucrative appointment in the Law Courts.

From now on we shall call his wife "Mrs. B."—that being the nickname which her Brooke grandsons later fastened on to her. She had quite a number of relations, and connections among the McCalmonts, the Bartons and her own people who were either rich (and so had houses that made useful ports of call and to which every year she made a round of visits) or who held good positions in which they were of use to her. Mrs. B. was very welcome in these houses, as she was witty and a good conversationalist, and could be trusted to make a party 'go'. One of the first things she instilled into her descendants was that it was their duty to do everything they could to help their host and hostess—that being the quickest way in which they could repay the hospitality they were receiving.

Having for long been accustomed to command and to issue orders, Mrs. B. received her first shake from my father, soon after my eldest brother Francis was born. She and my father had taken a house in Dublin for the event, and when the baby was about a month old Mrs. B. said that some particular actor was in Dublin that week, and they must all go to see him. My father at once said,

"Alma is not well enough to go to a theatre".

Mrs. B. said "And why not? She was always well enough to go to a theatre before she was married".

To which my father retorted, "She never had a baby before she was married". And Mrs. B. was left speechless.

Her son, Jimmie McCalmont, who was in the room at the time, never having heard anything like this before, thoroughly enjoyed himself.

Mrs. B. inspired in her grandchildren a good deal of awe, not to say fear, though she herself had a wholesome respect for my mother, and if my mother was anywhere in the offing, Mrs. B. restrained herself. The only encounter that I personally remember having had with her was in the Shelbourne Hotel, where she was spending the winter while a house she had bought was being put in order for her. Some of us were sent in to Dublin to lunch with Mrs. B. and she duly announced that as a treat and as something new, she would take us up in the lift. I took one look at the lift, was seized with a feeling of claustrophobia and said . . . I would *not* go up in it. This was not to be tolerated and I was ordered in, but got past her and fled up the stairs with Mrs. B. in hot pursuit. I was seven years old—she was sixty-seven.

I beat her right up to the top and if I had only realised that there was another way down I would have reached the bottom again without being caught, but I went down a passage where I was cornered, brought back again and forced into the lift which was obediently standing where we had left it.

I was most indignant and so was Mrs. B. at being defied by a small boy and drawn into this extraordinary hunt in the Shelbourne Hotel where many of the guests, and of course all of the staff, knew her quite well.

She was a firm believer in the maxim that children should be seen but not heard, but with the knowledge that my mother was in the background, she had to take a good deal more from us than she would have done in the case of her own children. Once when some of us were stopping with her in Dublin she came in to the Nannie and asked if there was anything wanted for the children as she was about to go out shopping. The Nannie said, "Please would you tell the grocer, Ma'm, to send in some biscuits".

Whereupon my brother, Augustine, shocked her by piping up—"And let them be cweam cwackers".

The same day at lunch Mrs. B. said, "Augustine, there's rice pudding and apple tart—which will you have?"

"I'll have *both* please".

"Then you'll be a very greedy little boy", and she felt she had got her own back—but he got *both* all the same.

She told Aunt Rose that she could not understand why Alma spoilt her children in the way she did. *She* had never done anything like that—a statement which Aunt Rose knew to be completely accurate.

Mrs. B. was very proud of her two sons and two daughters —my mother on account of her undoubted good looks, and Aunt Rose for her talent as a painter in water colours. Rose was a member of the old Water Colour Society and most of her work consisted of drawings of London. She wrote "Familiar London" published by A. & C. Black which was entirely illustrated by her pictures. Her drawings were first-class and

EMILY, MRS. JAMES McCALMONT (AFTERWARDS MRS. AUGUSTINE BARTON), 1827-1907.
WITH HER PONIES "SINNER" AND "SAINT"

(Painted by her sister, Elizabeth Kennedy)

as she always made an accurate as well as an attractive picture of whatever street she was painting, her work will some day be of value as an historical record of the London that changes so rapidly from year to year.

Mrs. B.'s elder son was Major General Sir Hugh McCalmont, K.C.B. and the younger, James, was Member of Parliament for North Antrim. James was not distinguished in debate but was an ideal Member from his Party's point of view, as there was never the slightest suggestion of a risk of his not being re-elected. In fact after his first election he was only opposed once during the twenty-five years in which he held his seat.

One of his constituents said of him "He's the right kind of a Member. He doesn't waste his time fiddlin' around at West-menster. If you want our Jemmie ye'll find him where he *should* be, warmin' his backside in front of the fire in the Ulster Club, and if you want anything done and its anny way possible at all, our Jemmie'll get it done for ye".

Having a son an M.P. even if not a very vocal one at West-minster, and other friends, English and Irish in both Houses, Mrs. B. took a lively interest in politics and was full of entertaining (and quite often accurate) gossip about what was going on, at a time when politics for Irish people was beginning to get very near the bone. She wrote in February 1893 about a debate in the House of Commons on Gladstone's second Home Rule Bill. Jimmie McCalmont had been ill and she starts by showing that he is better;

"I saw him in his place in the House this afternoon. I was lucky in getting there to-day as there was a row with the Irish brigade which lasted some time and caused the G.O.M. to speechify, and Col. Saunderson[1] had his say, also Mr. Balfour. Dunbar[2] floundered into some irrelevant matter and was called

---

[1] Colonel Edward Saunderson, leader of the Irish Unionist Party.
[2] Her nephew, Dunbar Barton, Q.C., Solicitor General for Ireland and Member for Mid Armagh. Afterwards Mr. Justice Barton, Judge of the Chancery Division in Dublin.

6

to order by the Speaker. Sat down, got up again, said something and again sat down by order, but there was such a din
of order and cheers I could not hear. The brogues of the
brigade were something awful and set the ladies laughing.
Davitt wore an old brown soft sort of Donnybrook hat. Gladstone looks shrunk to nothing since I saw him last. He reminded
me of Dick Bushe[1] and is as colourless. He looked like a
demon during Lord Randolph's speech which was a fine one
at times. Very amusing and sarcastic and his wind-up about
Ulster was grand. The Prince of Wales was there and the
Duke of York. I went at 2.30 and did not leave until Lord R.'s
speech ended at 7.30". Showing her eagerness to find out as
much as she could about anything that was likely to interest
her, the letter ends—"The housemaid at our lodgings is
daughter to the keeper of the Queen's stables and he has sent
me an order to go and see them. Love to all. Yr. loving Ma".

When Mrs. B.'s season in London came to an end she
usually made her way back to Ireland via Scotland where
she stayed at Mauldslie Castle in Lanark, with Lord Newlands,
whose wife had been Fannie O'Hara from Raheen in Galway,
and a cousin of Mrs. B. She generally stayed there for some
time and usually there were some other Irish people in the
party. One, Freddie Lawless[2], was a noted performer on the
piano, which his friends said was never quite the same instru-
ment again after Freddie had finished beating it. Just before
one of his visits, Lord Newlands had bought a new grand
piano from some celebrated maker and after dinner Miss
Hosier, Lord Newlands' daughter, suggested that Mr. Lawless
might play for them. Of course everyone including Lord
Newlands was delighted—or said so—but when they went to
open the piano it was locked and there was no key! Miss Hosier
hunted all over the room for it, and Lord Newlands said that

---

[1] A relation of her father's second wife, almost legendary in Kildare Street
Club for what was known as "Dick Bushe's Cough".
[2] Afterwards the last Lord Cloncurry.

the piano had not been opened since the makers delivered it —and he could only think that they had by mistake taken the key away with them. Then Mrs. B. caught his eye and he signalled to her to come over to him.

He said "They'll never find it. It's here (patting his trousers pocket). I'm not going to have Freddie breaking up my piano before anyone else has had a chance to play on it". Mrs. B. was much gratified at this sign of his confidence in her discretion.

On another occasion when Aunt Rose was also staying at Mauldslie, the men came in after dinner with a good deal of laughter and chaff, because one of them had picked up a garter from the dining-room floor. It was not a fancy one, but quite ordinary, so it was decided it must belong to a housemaid.

When the time came to go to bed, Aunt Rose went with Mrs. B. to her room for a short chat, and to her amazement as soon as the door was shut, Mrs. B. took the mate of the garter off her leg and threw it into the fire. Aunt Rose said . . . "But Mama! *you* made more jokes about it than anyone".

"Well, surely you would not expect me to claim a thing like that in front of all the gentlemen".

This was in the days when ladies' legs, generally speaking, were not talked about at all, much less their garters.

Mrs. B. generally came home via Inver House where she had first met James McCalmont and where now lived her sister Mary who had married Tom Barklie, he having succeeded to the place. She then did a kind of autumn season in Dublin, entertaining a good deal, being very fond of whist and later on of bridge, and she was an equally bad player at both games. She always spent Christmas at Summerton, then went back to Dublin to continue her season there.

She had a cabman named Farrell whom she employed. He had a good horse and a well-found cab, as well as an outside car. Years after her death (which took place in 1907)

I wanted a car one day in Dublin and having hailed one found to my great delight that the driver was Farrell. Of course we began at once to discuss the old days and Mrs. B. in particular. Farrell asked if I remembered the Big Wind.[1]

"Well, that night, I had her over the other side of the Square, playin' cards, and she came out and says she, 'Farrell', says she 'go back home and tell Kate to give you me glasses, off the table in me room. I'm after losing five pounds and I don't want to lose any more'. So I got the glasses and when she came out to go home she said 'I'm after winnin' back me fiver and a bit more, for when I had me glasses I could see the cards'. And the wind blew th'ould cab around the Square and I took her out of it in me arms and the wind blew the two of us down the Square and I had Hell's delight to get her into the house".

She had indeed all sorts of theories about luck at cards. Probably the spectacles were exactly the same as the ones she already had with her, but she thought the change of glasses would change the luck. I have seen her in her own house when she was holding bad cards, get up and in order to change the luck, throw the pack into the fire. But in this she was not peculiar; there is an entry in an old minute book of the

---

[1]This was a storm, always so-called, which occurred in February 1903. Whole roofs were blown away in Dublin and many people were hurt. In the Phoenix Park the magnificent avenue of elms along the Polo Ground, planted by the Earl of Chesterfield in the early 18th century, was completely swept away.

One of the cellarmen (Bill Butterly by name) employed by Thompson D'Olier & Co. Ltd., where I was Managing Director, used to be drawn by the other men to tell them about this storm. He lived in a very old house in Bridgefoot Street. He was a confirmed celibate and was looked after by his Aunt whom he always alluded to as "th' oul ant". Bill said, "Ye'd hear the wind comin' up howling and roarin' till it hit th' oul house a crack that shook it and honest to God ye'd think it'd come down on top of you. Then th' oul ant took fright and nuttin'd quite (quiet) her till I got into the bed wid her".

The same man, at the height of the worst blitz of London during the last war, remarked, "This man Tickler seems to be causin' a gradle (great deal) of annoyance".

Committee of Kildare Street Club which runs:—

> "Reported that the Earl of Milltown tore up and
> burnt a pack of cards. Ordered that his Lordship pay
> the cost of two packs of cards to replace the pack he
> destroyed by tearing it up and burning it in the fire".

Mrs. B.'s last outings, of which there are records, were in
connection with the Coronation of King Edward VII. She
was then seventy-seven. On the day of the Coronation she
started out from her lodgings to walk to the House of Commons
stand at Westminster to see the Coronation Procession. What
impressed her most were the State carriages of the Peers
"and their occupants, quite splendid". She sat in her place
for five hours, then went to the House of Commons for lunch
and tea on the terrace, and Jimmie McCalmont brought her
back to her lodgings at six o'clock in the evening. Then
during the celebrations she went down for the last day of
Cowes Regatta. Apparently she came down from London
by an early train and was met at Portsmouth.

"We were a party of twelve in a *small* launch, it was rough
beyond words. Edith[1] was frightened and thought we were
lost and certainly we rolled about in a most uncomfortable
if not dangerous style. Mrs. St. Leger and her friend Mrs.
Lambton *fainted* and Major St. Leger was very ill. I had not
a feather ruffled and Colonel Haine and Cuthbert said I was
grand. I think I was too excited to be bad. The ladies were
laid down but the boat rocked so it was a work of the greatest
difficulty to get a little brandy down their throats. Edith was
only frightened, not ill. We were an hour and a half going
over and we should have done it in half the time. However
we had a pleasant tea in the Yacht Club gardens, remained
late to see the illuminations which were lovely and then came
back to Portsmouth, the wind gone down and what there was
after us. Colonel Haine had champagne and sandwiches

---

[1] Her step-sister, Mrs. Cuthbert Dawson, whom she rather disliked.

for us and we did not arrive at Portsmouth until after 12.00. They have asked me to go back and see the Naval Review on Saturday next".

Not the least interesting part of this letter is the postmark. The date is Aug. 11. '02, 12.15 a.m. London. It was delivered at Castleknock at 5.40 p.m. the same day and was delivered into the house at Summerton, seven miles from Dublin, by 7 p.m. There was no motor delivery then, but it would take fifteen hours longer now, fifty-nine years later, and the delay is not altogether in Ireland.

Having described Mrs. B.'s life right to the end I must now go back to earlier times in order to give an account of those belonging to her. As already told she married Augustine Barton, their wedding having taken place in 1853. In due course two daughters were born to them—Alma (my mother), in October 1854, and Rose (Aunt Rose) in April 1856. These two, as might be gathered from what has gone before, were strictly brought up by their mother, to the extent that Aunt Rose was always relieved if she got past the door of the drawing-room in the house in Fitzwilliam Square, without her mother hearing and calling her in. It must not be thought from this that she was not fond of her mother—she was indeed extremely fond—but Mrs. B. immediately observed any lapse in the way her daughters were turned out, or any fault in their appearance in general and was wont to call strict attention to the matter. She had what might nowadays be thought somewhat odd views on diet and always made her baby daughters drink Guinness's Stout—saying it was good for the complexion. They had a French maid when they were small and at an early age my mother spoke French fluently. During a very bad crossing to Dover, at the age of about three, she was heard announcing— "Personne que le bon Dieu peut nous sauvir maintenant".

Later they had a German Governess, were taught drawing, and both played the piano creditably, so that everything was done to equip them well in the accomplishments in which young ladies of the day were expected to be proficient. In addition they played whist well, Aunt Rose particularly so. She generally held good cards so was much sought after as a partner. Always a good player she enjoyed piquet, whist and, later on, bridge right to the end of her life. She was also proficient at backgammon and when she was old it was very amusing to watch a hardened player—thinking that here was an old lady who was fair game—grow surprised to find herself gammoned twice in three games and with quite a bit to pay at the end of the evening. Aunt Rose also liked having a bet on a horse, and as her executor I had to pay her bookie £3 on the Monday after her death.

When they were young, their mother (Mrs. B.) always took them with her when she went to stay with relations and friends, and as they grew up they went with her to all the ports of call on her rounds of visits; all this very probably, it must be admitted, with an eye on how useful these houses might be to her when the girls would have grown up. Their father never went with them on the rounds. He was not always in the best of health and neither hunted nor shot as he grew older. He preferred the comfort and warmth of his house in Dublin, whist and billiards, and the company of his many friends in Kildare Street Club. During those weeks when the Club was annually closed for cleaning and redecoration, he was always restless and querulous—and his family was delighted when the Club opened again.

The two daughters came out and were presented in 1872, during Lord Spencer's first term of office as Lord Lieutenant. The earliest grown-up photograph of my mother is dated 1872 when she was eighteen, and her gown was described as a "Venetian dress", which she wore in a quadrille organised by Lady Olive Guinness, afterwards Lady Ardilaun, at a dance at the Castle.

Augustine Barton died in 1874, and being in mourning my

grandmother and her two daughters went abroad and spent most of the winter in Brussels, where they had drawing and painting lessons from people who were said to be the best masters available. They then went on up the Rhine and so to Switzerland. At Geneva they found John Hatchell, a friend from Dublin, and to make the money go farther, he and my grandmother went shares in hiring the carriage in which they went for drives. Dublin was at that time a hot-bed of gossip and it was impossible to do anything, anywhere, without an account of it coming back to the town by the Liffey. When therefore Mrs. B. and the girls returned, they were amazed to find that John Hatchell and my grandmother were reported about to be married, and furthermore, most people considered that in marrying again so soon after Augustine Barton's death, she was not displaying the best of taste. However the lady was well able to deal with the gossips who had been spreading such news!

They took up the round of gaiety again in the next season in Dublin and in London, and then made all their country visits in England and Ireland. In addition to dances and dinner-parties in Dublin, and a succession of private theatricals which were then much in fashion, there were Hunt Balls in the country, and Aunt Rose did a certain amount of hunting. In fact, by their own account they had a very good time. As regards my mother, the last season of this kind she had was in 1881, when she became engaged to my father. They were married in April of that year.

Not long afterwards Aunt Rose had an unfortunate love affair. The young man had got heavily into debt and his family said that before any arrangements could be made he must go overseas and remain away until he had righted his finances. Aunt Rose, however, never saw him again, for in less than six months he had contracted some type of fever and died. She then decided to work professionally at her painting, which she did most successfully — and from the end of the 1880's, when she got properly started, until well into the 1920's, she earned considerable sums of money by the sale of her water-colours at exhibitions, and at several very successful one-man shows of her own.

6. *Pomp and Circumstance*

THE Dublin Castle Season, as will have been seen from the last chapter, was a period of great gaiety, during which there was much entertaining of every kind and it was the means of circulating a great deal of money in the country. The Season began with a levee and a Drawing Room in Dublin Castle in the first week of February, and came to an end with the Saint Patrick's Ball on the evening of Saint Patrick's Day, 17th March, six weeks later.

The levee took place at 11.30 a.m., and all the men who wished to pay their respects to the Sovereign's Representative assembled in the long Drawing Room overlooking the Upper Castle Yard, the soldiers in uniform, the Bench and Bar in their robes and wigs and levee dress with knee breeches and silk stockings, Deputy Lieutenants in their uniforms of scarlet coatee with silver lace embroidered with shamrocks, and private people in black velvet court suits. All were ushered into the Throne Room, where the Lord Lieutenant was standing in front of the Throne accompanied by the Commander of the Forces and the Chief Secretary for Ireland (if Parliament was not sitting), and attended by his household and staff. The State Steward, Comptroller, Master of the Horse, Private Secretary, and any aides-de-camp who were not actually in waiting were grouped on his left. Cards with the respective names were handed to the aide-de-camp who passed them on up to the Chamberlain standing on the Lord Lieutenant's right and he read out the names. A bow was made to the Lord Lieutenant and the courtier walked through and out of the Throne Room.

The Drawing Room took place on the following evening at ten o'clock. It took quite a long time for a carriage finally to reach the Castle; it got into what was called the String. There were two strings, one from the west followed the South Quays, and the other from the east came up Dame Street, and those privileged people, peeresses, wives of judges and Privy Councillors and such-like who had the entrée, went round the back of the Castle and came in by the Ship Street gate. All the rest came in by the Upper Castle Yard, four carriages being allowed in at a time from each string. A carriage might be anything up to an hour in the string, moving forward a small distance at a time at a walk. The "Shawlies" of Dublin thoroughly enjoyed the evening. The windows of the carriages had to be opened for ventilation and these ladies walked along gazing into the carriages and making comments —often of refreshing candour—about the occupants. Aunt Grace said that on one occasion a woman had a good look at her and then called to her friend, "Mary, come and look at this one. Look at the bulgy eyes of her" and another looked in at my Mother and said,

"Ah! I like this one. She's so plain".

This did not mean an aspersion on her looks, but was a compliment because she appeared to be a good mixer and had laughed at whatever original comment had been made. The extraordinary thing was that there never appeared to be any police about, except actually at the Castle and there must have been many thousands of pounds worth of diamonds in the carriages along the strings.

The ladies wore full dress with court trains, feathers and lappets, and all the diamonds they possessed. The men wore full Court dress. Generally this was the same as the levee dress, but there were exceptions, notably Privy Councillors who wore the blue coatees buttoned up to the throat with magnificent gold embroidery in front, and white knee breeches and silk stockings, and the vice regal staff who also wore blue cutaway coats with white knee breeches and silk stockings and any gold lace was entirely of gold shamrocks. Everybody moved slowly through the long drawing room and when they reached the door of the Throne Room, footmen took the trains off the ladies' arms and spread them out. The ladies then walked round to where (as at the levee) the Lord Lieutenant was standing in front of the Throne with his wife beside him. Their cards went up and the Chamberlain read out the name —and if a girl was being presented, the name of the lady presenting her was also read out.

The men escorting the ladies just walked through at the back and met them at the other door where footmen were re-arranging the trains. They then went into the picture gallery where there was a buffet supper. They were supposed then to wait until the ladies had all been through, when the Lord Lieutenant with his wife, all his staff walking in front, and their house party two and two behind, went in state through St. Patrick's Hall to the Privy Council room at the far end which was his private supper room.

The portraits of past Lord Lieutenants in the picture gallery were crabbed by most people and Dunbar Barton, who was on the Duke of Marlborough's staff, told me that when the Duke's portrait was hung it fell to him to take the Duchess in to see it. She just looked at it, said "The buttons are excellent" and walked away.

If any of the Royal Family were present the ladies curtseyed to them as well as to the Lord Lieutenant and his wife, so that when the Duke of Connaught was Commander of the Forces they had to make seven curtseys; to the Lord Lieutenant and his wife, the Duke and Duchess of Connaught, Prince Arthur and the two Princesses. There was a second levee and a second Drawing Room half way through the season, but the numbers at these were usually small.

The entertaining included three large dinner-parties each week, and on Tuesdays and Thursdays there were dances in the Throne Room. At these the soldiers wore mess kit and the civilians ordinary evening dress. There were two State Balls in St. Patrick's Hall when full uniform was worn by soldiers and court dress by the civilians, and finally there was the Saint Patrick's Ball on the evening of Saint Patrick's Day, which brought the season to an end. This was a very entertaining affair. Instead of the State Quadrille with which all the other dances and balls were opened, there was a sort of Country Dance, which was very gay and gave you the impression that you might be back in the eighteenth-century, and there was a tradition that it dated back as far as that and had always been danced on Saint Patrick's Night. There was a certain likeness to Sir Roger de Coverley, but it was different in that the dancers did not go round outside the lines and so move up, but they dropped back into their places and the next couples came forward. It was not a reel nor yet a jig. The dancers were in two long lines facing each other, about twenty couples. The Lord Lieutenant opened the dance with the wife of the Chamberlain. They came tripping out to meet each other and did some small figure in the centre and back into their places, and then the Chamberlain danced with the wife of the Lord

Lieutenant, and all the other couples came through in the same way; the dancers that stood gradually further from the centre having further to go before they met their partner in the centre. It was danced to all the old Irish jigs, "St. Patrick's Day", "The Hare in the Corn", "Drops of Brandy" and the "Huntsman's Jig". It was not walked like the Quadrille, but had its own style of steps which can only be described as tripping along to the tune and time of the jigs.

Saint Patrick's Hall made a splendid setting for a big ball, with its white and gold decorations, its painted ceiling and the banners of the Knights of Saint Patrick. The guests at all the balls were asked for ten o'clock and at two a.m. the Band played "God Save the King" and the Lord Lieutenant then made his bow to his guests, who bowed and curtseyed and he proceeded out of the Ballroom with his house party and his staff and the ball was over.

In addition to the Castle entertaining there was a great deal of private entertaining—dinner parties and dances as well as large subscription dances for charities held, in the Pillar Room at the Rotunda. The ballroom of the old Assembly Rooms there had a beautiful floor for dancing.

One particular year, twenty young men clubbed together to give what they called "The Bachelors' Ball". They had to postpone it from the original date fixed, owing to the Vice-regal Court being put into mourning by the death of the Duke of Cambridge. One of the Committee had taken it into his head to insure against any postponement and with the extra money they spread themselves. They brought over Iff's band from London and in addition to the Ballroom and small supper room, hired the large Supper Room upstairs and for "sitting out" the Round Room.[1] The rooms were all decorated with flowers by Mrs. Swan who was noted for work of this

---

[1] The "Round Room" or Rotunda, which gave its name to the assembly rooms and to the Hospital which owned them. *The Rotunda Hospital.* C. P. Curran. Dublin 1945.

kind, and in the centre of the Round Room she arranged an enormous block of ice so that the heated dancers might be able to cool themselves. As a great entertainment, it was a last revival of those brilliant functions which in the days before the Union helped to provide the income of the Rotunda Hospital.

What might be called the general ritual of the Dublin Season, as just described, had gone on without much change for many years and went on to the end, but under different Viceroys, and as fashions changed the general forms of outside entertainment and amusement varied over the years. During the 1870's there was a run of private theatricals and a number of fancy dress balls. One show was a pantomime of "Blue Beard", in which my Mother took the part of Fatima, and several of the other chief parts were taken by her near relations. Her half-brother, Jimmie McCalmont, then a Captain in the 8th Hussars, and who seems to have been on the staff of each Lord Lieutenant in turn, was Sister Anne whilst her cousin, Major Robert Barklie of Inver, was Blue Beard. They put on "H.M.S. Pinafore" on another occasion, which cannot have been very long after its original production. Jimmie McCalmont was Admiral Porter and my Mother was one of the nieces in the chorus. At that time there was always a Battalion of Guards in Dublin and they usually gave a Ball during the Season and one notable fancy dress Ball.

After the Castle Season the Lord Lieutenant moved out to the Viceregal Lodge in the Phoenix Park. He entertained there in an informal way and usually had large parties for Punchestown and the Horse Show. At Punchestown they drove up the Course and were received at the gate into the enclosure by the Master of the Kildare Hounds and members of the Kildare Hunt.

During the summer there were cricket matches on the cricket grounds of the Viceregal Lodge, and usually a cricket week when there were three two-day matches. The Zingari often brought a side, and the Na Shuler, and one year there was an Old Wykehamist side. In 1887 it is recorded that there was a match between the Viceregal and Mr. Mahaffy's side. (Mr. Mahaffy was afterwards Sir John Pentland Mahaffy, K.C.V.O., Provost of Trinity College.) It was a one-day match and the Provost's side (one cannot call him by any other name) won on the first innings with three wickets to spare. He did not play himself but his son Arthur did and on the Viceregal side Captain Fowler made 39 not out. He was father of Bob Fowler whose name will always be associated with the historic Eton and Harrow match of 1910—Fowler's Match.

Probably the Viceregal Court and the Dublin Castle Season were at their zenith in the ten years from 1895 to 1905, particularly in the first seven when Lord Cadogan was Lord Lieutenant. He kept great state and all his and Lady Cadogan's appearances in public, and their entertainments, both at the Castle and the Viceregal Lodge, were conspicuous for the dignity with which they were carried out. They inherited from their predecessors as Chamberlain, Sir Gerald Dease and as Master of the Horse, Colonel Frank Foster, who had ridden in the Charge of the Heavy Brigade at Balaclava, and had been Master of the Horse to the Duke of Marlborough in 1876. He held the office until 1902 when he retired.

When the Duke of Marlborough was Lord Lieutenant, the Empress of Austria came to Ireland, more than once, to hunt in Meath. Of course she was in Ireland incognito, but the Duchess of Marlborough was slightly jealous that another star should appear in the firmament. At the end of one of the Empress's visits, some of those who had been hunting with her in Meath (including Colonel Foster), arranged to give her a small dinner at the Royal St. George Yacht Club at Kingstown before she went on board the Mail Boat. Two days before this dinner party, Colonel Foster was disconcerted at receiving an intimation that he would be expected to dine at the Castle on the same night. He knew that if he

GEORGE FREDERICK BROOKE, 1849-1926
First Baronet of Summerton
(From the painting by Sir William Orpen, R.A.)

remained away from this function, the Duchess would be certain to find out the reason. Rather than face the ensuing complications, the Colonel decided that as it could feasibly be done in the time, the only solution was to eat *both* dinners —and this he did.

With long training in the management of the Viceregal stables, and being able to keep on the postilions and out-riders from one change of Lord Lieutenant to another, together with the knowledge Colonel Foster had acquired of stables in London which jobbed big black carriage horses of the type he wanted, with a Lord Lieutenant such as Lord Cadogan behind him prepared to spend money on horses—with all this, he was enabled to produce carriages, horses and the right sort of trained servants, to make an absolutely first-class turnout. Lord Cadogan's colours were pale blue, the footmen at the Castle wore blue and silver state liveries. The carriages had a light blue line on the wheels and panels, and the horses light blue head bands and knots.

During Lord Cadogan's Viceroyalty there were many events of a kind unknown for a long time. First in 1897 the Duke and Duchess of York paid a visit, driving in state in the Viceregal carriages to the Viceregal Lodge where the Lord Lieutenant was in residence for the summer. The Lord Lieutenant took no part in the State entry. As the Queen's Representative, he took precedence in Ireland of everyone, even the Prince of Wales had he come over, and the Duke of York. When they all drove in State to the Horse Show, the Lord Lieutenant and Lady Cadogan drove in the first carriage, while the Duke and Duchess of York followed in the second.

My brothers and I went with my Mother to the Kildare Street Club to see the Duke and Duchess of York's state entry, but on arrival at the Club she was told by the Secretary, Mr. Bailey, with much regret on his part, that the Committee had given instructions that no schoolboys were to be allowed

93

7

in. So we went out to see what we could see from the footpath in Nassau Street in front of the club. About ten minutes later Mr. Bailey appeared and told us to come in. He said that Lord Monck, a Member of the Committee, had arrived with his ten year old son, George, and had brought him in saying that the order was quite ridiculous, and if he had been present at the Committee meeting he would never have allowed it to be passed. So we went in, but in the meantime George Monck on coming into the morning-room spied his Aunt, Lady Rachel Saunderson, seated in a corner. He made a charge at her—and before anyone could stop him, delivered her a terrific blow in the stomach. Luckily the plate armour of her stays protected her and so no great harm was done.

George Monck was a first-class chap and when we grew up he was a very dear friend of mine. He unfortunately early contracted T.B. and died when he was about twenty-five.

While they were staying at the Viceregal Lodge, the Duke and Duchess of York were in the habit of going out on their bicycles in the Phoenix Park before breakfast. One morning when some way from home the Duchess of York's bicycle had a puncture. A young man who was passing offered to help and mended the puncture for her. When he had finished, the Duke of York remarked to the lad that the lady whose tyre he had repaired was the Duchess of York, his wife.

Whereupon the young man said, "Ha! Ha!, is she? Well I'm Kaiser William!" and got on his bicycle and rode away.

Then there was the Queen's last visit to Ireland in the spring of 1900, less than a year before she died, when many people thought that the Royal Horses and Carriages did not compare favourably with those of the Viceregal procession.

During the last years of Lord Cadogan's term of office the Duke of Connaught was at the Royal Hospital as Commander of the Forces in Ireland, and he and the Duchess entertained largely, helping to make Lord Cadogan's Viceroyalty the splendid period it was. In addition to the more important entertaining there were afternoon parties at the Royal Hospital for hockey in which the Duchess and the Princesses took part.

We had hockey parties of a humbler nature at Summerton and at one of them considerable sensation was caused when a girl, due to be presented at the Castle three nights later, was hit in the eye by a ball, and was sent home to her mother with a raw beef-steak tied to her eye by a white bandage. It was said that the steak, being applied at once, did what was required and the appearance of the victim when she was presented did great credit to the home doctoring. Unkind people said that the Summerton hockey was very violent, not to say dangerous, and that there was only one rule—the players were not allowed to bite, and furthermore if this rule was infringed the punishment was that the biter was to be bitten by the bittee who held on until the umpire said "Hold! enough!"

Lord Cadogan retired in 1902 and was succeeded by Lord Dudley. His term of office was also very splendid, but people thought his Court was flashy in comparison to the solid state of Lord Cadogan's régime.

While Lord Dudley was Lord Lieutenant, King Edward paid his State Coronation visit to Dublin, Belfast and Cork, and it was after this visit that among the Honours, my father was created a Baronet. The King held a levee in the Castle, and also with Queen Alexandra, a Court in Saint Patrick's Hall in the Castle. All the Irish people who had wished to attend a Drawing Room in London had been told that the King would be holding a Court later on in Dublin, and it was his wish that they should come to it, so it was a very large and magnificent affair. The guests, instead of waiting in the long drawing room, sat in Saint Patrick's Hall, leaving space around the thrones for the actual presentations, so that everyone got a magnificent view of the Royal Procession and the King and Queen taking their seats on the Thrones. My Mother, who was there, said that when the Queen was seated and her train had been arranged by her pages, the Mistress of the Robes, the Duchess of Buccleuch, blazing with diamonds and almost as magnificent a figure as the Queen herself, came forward and while the pages stood on one side, re-arranged the Queen's train more to her satisfaction.

After the visit to the three cities was over the King made an informal tour of Connemara, which was a tremendous success, and in that country stamped the King forever as a very great gentleman. Queen Alexandra charmed everyone and children presented her with bouquets wherever she went. She and the King left their car and walked up in the rain to visit the people in their cottages and in one a feeble old woman offered her a little bouquet of white and purple heather with a prayer for a long life.[1]

We too had our rejoicings at Summerton, in celebration of my father's baronetcy. He and my mother and I were sitting in the drawing room after dinner when Kynes[2] came in and said that Mr. West was at the hall door to say that some of the neighbours had lighted a bonfire at the gate and they hoped that Sir George and Lady Brooke would come down and meet them. So the three of us set out, I as a spectator of course, feeling a certain amount of responsibility in that I would be expected to give an account of the proceedings to the brothers who were away from home. Mr. George West was one of two brothers who had successful market gardens on the Strawberry Beds.

When we arrived at the gate, George West made a speech congratulating my Father and Mother, and in the peroration with which he wound up, he said that King Edward was the beautifullest monarch that ever adorned the British Throne and his beautifullest deed was creating Sir George a Baronet. My father who was a good deal moved, made a short reply Nearly all those assembled there were much the same age as

---

[1]"Memories, wise and otherwise" Sir Henry Robinson, London 1923, page 154.
[2]The Butler.

himself, and as he had known them all since they had been boys, he was greatly touched by this mark of their appreciation. He and my mother then walked round and shook hands with everyone. She was splendid, as things were becoming rather tense, and by making a pleasant remark to each in turn as she went round she kept things moving, until at the exact psychological moment Kynes appeared, with the footman and pantry-boy following, each carrying two large bedroom hot water cans filled with beer. Then things were well away.

My father had probably given him a hint before he left the house, but in any case on an occasion of that sort Kynes could always be trusted to produce what was wanted at the right moment.

Lord Dudley went out with the change of Government at the end of 1905 and was succeeded by Lord Aberdeen. Lord Aberdeen had already been a rather unsuccessful Lord Lieutenant for a few months in 1886 and indeed it could not have been easy to follow the splendid ten years that had just come to an end. In the first place, both his predecessors had been very rich men, and Lord Aberdeen was understood not to have that advantage; having this knowledge, therefore, people were quite prepared to recognise that there was likely to be a considerable curtailment of entertaining and ceremony, but what they were not prepared for was the Lord Lieutenant's utter lack of dignity.

He gave an impression of continually hopping from one leg to the other, his hands were never still for one moment, and he seemed always to be jerking his head from one side to the other, as if afraid that he might miss something. When he arrived at the Horse Show he took off his hat and put it on again, then quickly repeated the operation, rather like an artiste about to do a music hall turn. The Viceregal Lodge was in the Parish of Castleknock, and he and Lady Aberdeen came to church very often, which his fellow-parishioners appreciated very much. What they did not like, was his announcement later on that he was going to read the lessons. Lord Aberdeen had an unpleasant voice, he read badly and went through all his peculiar exercises in front of the lectern. The parishioners disliked it very much, but without being rude there was nothing they could do about it. The Church having been dis-established, his position as a member of the congregation was exactly the same as that of any other parishioner, but the Lord Lieutenant was, after all, the King's Representative and had to be treated as such, with due respect.

At the Castle Balls, Lord Aberdeen had a favourite dance in which he liked to take part. The band was instructed to play the tune and an A.D.C. led up the victim chosen to dance with the Lord Lieutenant. She always had a "Heaven-help-me" look on her face, such as Andromache might have had while she was waiting for Perseus, but no help came. She made her curtsey to the Lord Lieutenant who clasped her to the Star of the Thistle on his breast and off they capered in the Canadian Polka, the steps of which were quite unknown to anyone except the Lord Lieutenant. The victim's friends, both male and female, thoroughly enjoyed the turn, the females a little chastened by the feeling that it might be *their* turn next.

At first no one minded this, looking on the want of dignity with amusement tinged with a certain amount of regret, that ridicule was being cast on what was a great historic office, but after a few years when they had become more firmly entrenched, Lord and Lady Aberdeen (but particularly Lady Aberdeen) began to put forward their own pet schemes. While her schemes undoubtedly did good, Lady Aberdeen was quite without tact, and had no consideration for what the feelings of other people might be. If some did not mind being trampled on—others did—and they became more and more restive until, feeling that there was no reason why these two should ever go, many people gradually ceased attending the Viceregal Court. Dissatisfied comment, which was quite open, must have reached the Viceregal ears, and one of the Dublin newspapers published a parody on "The Wearing of the Green" of which three verses will be sufficient here;

"I met a Brother Paddy and I shook him by the hand
How are you all in Ireland and how does she stand?
Said he, the Farmers have the land and all can wear the green
But we've got the Curse of Scotland here in Lady Aberdeen.

Good luck to those who came before, the noble & the great,
Who ruled in Dublin Castle Halls in true Viceregal state.
Who wore the garter and the star with all their pomp & sheen
Not like the cringing feckless coon the Earl of Aberdeen.

Those were the days of Open Court, both plentiful & free
No niggard hand supplied the board that welcomed you & me
Where Lady Londonderry[1] stood & Spencer's Faerie Queen[2]
Another type of hostess stands, the Lady Aberdeen."

Lampoons of this kind were quite usual—directed towards British Statesmen and politicians, but not up till now at the Sovereign's Representative.

Finally, Lady Aberdeen committed a gaucherie which the Government could not overlook in the wife of the King's Representative.

When the 1914–18 War broke out, in Ireland as everywhere else collections were made for comforts for the troops and for the Red Cross. A Branch of the Red Cross, the County Dublin Branch, was set up in Dublin, with a Committee of well known ladies and gentlemen, and with Mr. Denis Pack-Beresford as Honorary Secretary. Lady Aberdeen had nothing to do with this Committee, and perhaps was jealous that an important and expanding branch of the British Red Cross

---

[1]Wife of 6th Marquis of Londonderry, Lord Lieutenant 1886–89.
[2]Wife of 5th Earl Spencer, Lord Lieutenant 1868–1874 & 1882–85.

Society should have been started in Dublin without her assistance or influence, but quite probably the Committee, knowing how determined she was to have her own way and to force the prestige of her position on to a committee of the kind, felt that the management would be more harmonious without her assistance.

To the general amazement, therefore, there appeared on the 17th October 1914 in 'Sinn Fein' a paper published weekly, a facsimile copy of a page of a letter purporting to have been written by Lady Aberdeen. It read as follows:—

Private.   Viceregal Lodge,
                                              Dublin.
                                    Sept. 20th 1914.
Dear Mr. Brayden,

I shall be grateful if you can put enclosed letter into a good place.

I am afraid there is a bit of a plot amongst the Unionists to capture the Red Cross Society in Ireland and to run it in such a way from London and through County Lieutenants and Deputy Lieutenants that will be unacceptable to the Irish Volunteer people etc.

Ishbel Aberdeen.

The rest of the letter, which was not on this facsimile page was printed, but it was mainly pointing out that if worked properly Lady Aberdeen and her friends could get an Irish Branch of the Red Cross going which would be entirely independent of the British Red Cross in London.

The signature had been cut out and pasted on to the facsimile reproduction to show that it was genuine.

The comment of the Editor of 'Sinn Fein' was,

"The letter, the first page of which we produce in

facsimile, occupies four pages. Mr. Brayden to whom
the letter is addressed is the Editor of the 'Freeman's
Journal' ".

On the 31st October, Mr. Denis Pack-Beresford, the Hon.
Secretary of the Executive Committee of the County Dublin
Branch of the British Red Cross Society asked the 'Irish Times'
to publish the correspondence that had passed between him
in his official capacity and Lady Aberdeen.

Dublin 20th October 1914

Dear Lady Aberdeen,

The Executive Committee of the County Dublin
Branch of the British Red Cross Society have seen in
two weekly papers—'The Irish Worker' and 'Sinn
Fein'—what purports to be a private letter over Your
Excellency's signature addressed to the Editor of the
'Freeman's Journal'. I am directed by my Committee
to communicate with Your Excellency on the
subject.

Your Excellency is made to appear as charging
a body of Irish men and Irish women with seizing
the occasion of a great public calamity to use the
Red Cross Society for political purposes. The fact
that the Society has the special patronage of Their
Majesties the King and Queen makes it almost
incredible that such a suggestion should be made
from the Viceregal Lodge. At the same time the serious effect likely to be produced by this letter upon
the work of one Branch in County Dublin and upon
that of other Branches throughout Ireland, makes my
Committee extremely anxious that Your Excellency
should take the earliest opportunity of publicly
disavowing its authenticity.

We venture to suggest that an announcement should be made in the Dublin newspapers, possibly in the form of a reply to this letter. We beg you to believe that nothing but our deep sense of the urgency of the matter and of the danger which threatens the welfare of the whole Red Cross Movement in Ireland could have induced us to bring this deplorable business to Your Excellency's notice.

Denis R. Pack-Beresford.
Hon. Secretary.

The Reply:—

Viceregal Lodge
Dublin.
Oct. 21st 1914.

Dear Mr. Pack-Beresford,

I beg to acknowledge receipt of your letter of yesterday's date.

In reply I can only say that, under the circumstances attending the appearance of the letter in question, I think it entirely unsuitable for me to discuss it in any way whatsoever.

Yours truly,
(Signed)   Ishbel Aberdeen.

and a further letter—

22nd October 1914

Dear Lady Aberdeen,

I beg to acknowledge the receipt of Your Excellency's letter of 21st inst.

I am directed to express the regret of this Executive

Committee that you cannot see your way to repudiate the authenticity of the letter in question. The Committee feel that under the circumstances the publication of the correspondence becomes necessary to show those interested in Red Cross work in Ireland that the Committee has done all in its power to minimise the injury caused by the publication of the letter. It is not intended however to send this correspondence to the Press until to-morrow.

Signed on behalf of the Executive Committee,

> Denis R. Pack-Beresford.
> Hon. Sec.

From Lady Aberdeen—

> Viceregal Lodge.
> Oct. 23 1914.

Dear Mr. Pack-Beresford,

I have duly received your letter of yesterday's date, but I can only again express surprise that it should be thought fitting, and in accordance with the recognised standards of fair dealing, that any notice should have been taken of a communication, the knowledge of which was acquired in the manner referred to.

As to the fact of further publication of correspondence, if this could be of any possible advantage to Red Cross work, of course, I would offer no objection, but I am afraid that it would be a case of the more publication the more harm to the work, especially if there were to be a discussion on the merits of the case.

> Yours very truly,
> (Sd.) Ishbel Aberdeen

103

On the 31st October 1914 the 'Irish Times' published a leading article:—

"The Public will read with profound regret the correspondence that has taken place between the County Dublin Branch of the British Red Cross Society and the Countess of Aberdeen. Lady Aberdeen virtually admits that she has accused Unionists of a plot to make political capital out of the sacred work of the Red Cross Society. Her refusal to satisfy the Society's request is capable of no other interpretation. She declines to disavow the authorship of the private letter to the Editor of the Freeman's Journal on the grounds that it was made public by unfair and disreputable means. That is of course perfectly true. A private letter was stolen we must assume from the person to whom it was addressed, and was published in two weekly newspapers. In ordinary circumstances no decent man or woman would gratify the authors of such a dirty trick by taking the slightest notice of it. But the circumstances in this case were not ordinary. A letter was attributed to the wife of the Lord Lieutenant which represented her as charging a body of Irish men and Irish women with an offence which at any time would be inconceivably base. On an occasion of this sort even the wife of the Lord Lieutenant cannot afford to stand on her dignity. Lady Aberdeen's duty was plain and instant. The County Branch of the Red Cross asked her to reconsider the refusal, but she declined to consider it. The Branch withheld the publication of the correspondence for a week, during which time the disavowal—if it were at all feasible—could have been made through any of the innumerable channels which are open to Her Excellency. It has not been made and only one

conclusion is possible. The private letter is genuine.
Lady Aberdeen charges a large body of Irish ladies
and gentlemen with a "plot to capture the Red
Cross Society of Ireland, and run it in such a way
that it will be unacceptable to the Irish Volunteer
people." By whom is this political charge made and
what does it mean? It is made by the wife of the one
man in Ireland whose strict duty and high privilege
it is to stand aloof from party politics. It means that
Lady Aberdeen holds a Society of Irish ladies and
gentlemen guilty of the use of a great public calamity
for political purposes. Our soldiers, English and Irish,
are fighting and dying in France. Many of them
wounded and maimed are now lying in Dublin
Hospitals. It is the duty of the Red Cross Society—a
proud and willing duty—to minister to the needs of
these gallant men in sickness and in health. The
Society comforts them in the battlefield, heals their
wounds, makes death easier for the dying. Lady
Aberdeen's charge is that Irish men and Irish women
in doing these things, are thinking chiefly of capturing
the Red Cross Society in the interests of Unionist
politics. It is a charge that, however sordidly it may
have been brought to light, these ladies and gentlemen
could not ignore. They resent it passionately. They
are profoundly astonished at one who wrote in the
'Irish Times'—'I am commanded by Queen
Alexandra, President of the British Red Cross Society,
to express Her Majesty's gratification of the response
that has already been made to the call for Red Cross
workers in Ireland'. The Red Cross Society in
Ireland embraces men and women of all creeds and
all political opinions. We believe that everyone of
them will resent Lady Aberdeen's charge, as those

against whom it is directed. The public of course requires no repudiation of it. The work of the Red Cross Society in Ireland since the beginning of the War speaks for itself. This unhappy incident will not be permitted to mar for a single moment the splendour of its unity and devotion".

The "Pall Mall Gazette" had—

"It is a melancholy little story, and it is not surprising that the influential public spirited men and women who control the Red Cross work in County Dublin bitterly resent Her Excellency's suggestion concerning the Society".

And the "Evening News"—

"Lady Aberdeen thinks it entirely unsuitable that she should discuss in any way whatever the publication of a private latter alleged to be written by her in which it is charged that the Unionists are engaged in a plot to capture the Red Cross Society in County Dublin. Perhaps her Ladyship is right. The letter is in grossly bad taste and the less said about it the better. Even if they are slandered, Unionists must go on working for the wounded".

It is curious that one so astute as Lady Aberdeen should have handled this affair so clumsily. It was perfectly obvious that she had written the letter and she did not actually deny having done so. If she had said at once in reply to Mr. Pack-Beresford's first letter, "Yes, I did write it" and at the same time protested at the way in which a private letter had found its way into the public press, and then remained quite silent, there was not very much more that Mr. Pack-Beresford and his Committee could have done. If he had written again all she had to say was, "I have answered the question you asked me, and I have nothing more to say on the matter".

It takes two sides to carry on an argument or a correspondence and that would probably have finished it all, so far as Dublin was concerned, but of course it might not have satisfied the Government nor perhaps the King, whose Representative Lord Aberdeen was in Ireland.

Lady Aberdeen's first reply to this correspondence was to establish about three weeks later a City of Dublin Branch of the *British* Red Cross, "British" being one of the objections she had to the County Branch. Of course she was at the head of it. Then three weeks later, it was announced that Lord Aberdeen had resigned "for private reasons".

There remained one more blunder for the Aberdeens to make and they made it. In the list of the New Year Honours on 1st January 1915 the Earl of Aberdeen gained the title of Marquis.

On the following 10th January there was a paragraph in the 'Irish Times'—

Marquis of Aberdeen and Tara

"The Times understands that Lord Aberdeen will assume the name of Tara with that of Aberdeen thus becoming the Marquis of Aberdeen and Tara.

The title of Tara is adopted to commemorate the long connection of Lord and Lady Aberdeen with Ireland and the Viceregal Office".

Instantly "the Harp that once" was taken down from Tara's walls and used for the accompaniment of a violent chorus of protest. On 19th January 1915 the 'Irish Times' had a paragraph.

"Tara as a Title

In a letter to The Times to-day Georgina Viscountess Gormanston[1] recalls that the title of Tara has already been held by two Irish Peers 'and I am not sure that the first one ever became extinct.' In 1650 Thomas Preston, fourth son of the fourth Viscount Gormanston was created Viscount Tara and John Preston of Bellinter was created Baron Tara at the time of the Union".

And on the same day there was a verse—

Ichabod

Once jewels decked the Knights who strode
In good Saint Patrick's Hall of Fame
And down through Ireland's ages glowed
The light of Tara's Kingly name
But now how sadly does she fare
How beggared is our Island Queen,
The jewels vanished[2]—Heaven knows where,
And Tara raped to Aberdeen.

On the 18th January the same paper had a leading article containing a good deal of heavy handed sarcasm:—

"Twice already has the name of Irish Tara appeared in the Peerage. In 1650 the Honourable Thomas

---

[1]She was the Mother of Viscount Gormanston, the head of the Preston family.

[2]This refers to the Crown Jewels of the Order of Saint Patrick which had been stolen not long before, and were never heard of again.

EMILY ALMA, LADY BROOKE, 1854-1910
(From the painting by Sir William Orpen, R.A.)

Preston fourth son of Christopher fourth Viscount
Preston was created Viscount Tara but the title
became extinct on the death of his grandson the
fifth Viscount. John Preston ... was created Baron
Tara in 1800, but on his death in 1821, without issue,
the title became extinct. Both the Preston's were Irish
and John Preston was the owner of part of the Hill
of Tara. How much greater is the compliment
which the name receives to-day from the annexation
by a Scottish Nobleman who does not own as much
of the soil of Tara as in the saying of the County
Meath peasantry, would sod a lark ... Lord
Aberdeen ... has taken the trouble of acquiring Lord
Gormanston's traditional rights in the title of 'Tara'
in order to rescue from livid oblivion a little hill in our
obscure midlands. If Tara had been a notable
place Lord Aberdeen's good taste and feeling would
have left it in undistinguished enjoyment of its
notability. If it had been crowned with sacred
memories, or a fountain of Irish history, or a home
of ancient Irish Kings or a jealously guarded temple
of the genius of Ireland—if in fact it had been a
peculiarly national possession—the new Scottish
Marquis would no more have thought of annexing it
than a new Irish Peer would think of taking his title
from Holyrood or Bannockburn. He has discovered
Tara for us just as the war has discovered La Bassee
and Lwow .... "

The "Daily Mail" said:—

"If it is difficult for an Englishman to do the right
thing in Ireland it is, possibly—we make the suggestion with great diffidence—even more difficult for a
Scotsman. Lord Aberdeen has served in Dublin for

nearly ten long if not particularly happy years. Yet they have not been long enough to initiate him into the elements of Irish thought and feeling. Honoured by the King on his resignation with a Marquisate he has chosen as his title 'Aberdeen and Tara'. So far from being grateful Irishmen are resentful when they see 'The theme of song, the hallowed shrine' used as gilding for a Scotch coronet. Great as Lord Aberdeen's services may have been, the general opinion is that they have not been so great as all that, and that they scarcely warrant his presumption in laying hands on a national possession. Perhaps when he is back in Scotland Lord Aberdeen may become conscious of a certain historic incongruity. Perhaps he may even be induced to choose some other title".

'The Times' made the same suggestion. Lord Aberdeen acted on it and it was announced that the title would be *Marquis of Aberdeen and Temair*. Though it was only a distinction without a difference, everyone seemed satisfied except the lady who received from Lady Aberdeen a photograph of herself, in which there was also a dog, and which she signed "Ishbel Aberdeen and Temair". In thanking for the photograph, the lady ended her letter by writing "I suppose Temair is the name of the dog".

It was the custom for a Lord Lieutenant on his first arrival in Dublin to make a State entry which consisted of a procession, the streets being lined with troops, from Westland Row Station to Dublin Castle, where he was sworn in. In the same way, when he left Ireland for the last time, he departed in State and on each occasion the Directors of the City of Dublin Steampacket Company would place one of their mail steamers at his disposal.

On the day in February 1915 when the Aberdeens were to

make their state departure there was the usual procession: the streets were lined and on the footpaths the usual crowd of spectators was assembled to see the pageant.

After the Escort came the Lord Lieutenant on horseback accompanied by his staff. Then came the carriage, with Lady Aberdeen sitting bolt upright, a Kodak in her hand, with a red rubber tube and a bulb to press which worked the shutter. Holding it high up above her head, so that she could not have seen what she was photographing, she pressed the bulb, and as soon as she had reeled off the exposure she took another snap shot. All the time as the carriage passed by there was no waving of handkerchiefs, no cheering, just roars of laughter.

And so with this tragic burlesque—
"And Laughter holding both his sides"
the curtain was rung down[1] on a succession that had lasted two hundred years, of noblemen who had represented their Sovereign in Ireland and kept great state in Dublin Castle.

---

[1] There were three more Viceroys, Lords Wimborne, French and Fitzalan, but as they only covered six years between them they hardly count.

7. *Limen Amabile*

MY Mother was a very able woman. She was extremely religious, which I think enabled her to face serenely, as she did, the difficulties she had to meet from time to time. Until the last year or two of her life she never was rattled, which showed great self-control in one who had to manage a stepson, seven sons and two daughters of her own, and her servants, and supervise the housekeeping for the whole crowd.

When the house was full at Christmas time or during Horse Show Parties—she had upwards of twenty-six people to cater for, and she never at any time kept a "housekeeper" in the accepted sense of the word. My mother was very good-looking, well read and well informed, and in addition was musical, playing the piano quite well. While we were still at Pickering, when the establishment was much smaller, in addition to readings from the Bible she taught Francis,

Augustine and myself the beginnings of reading and writing. As well as hearing the Bible read, as part of our religious instruction we were provided with a large Old Testament picture book. The three pictures I remember best were— Elisha calling out to the bears to deal with the rude children (which the Nannie said ought to be a lesson to us)—Daniel in the lions' den, wherein Daniel in the right-hand bottom corner was sitting surrounded by lions and looking rather as if he was teaching them the alphabet, while in the top left-hand corner, Darius complete with crown was looking in to see if Daniel was all right. The third picture showed Absalom hanging by his hair, which was caught in the boughs of the oak. He looked very uncomfortable and in the background his mule was shown departing into the country at full gallop.

When we lived at Summerton the invariable custom after lunch on Sunday was for my father and mother to set out for a walk accompanied by anyone who had lunched with us, or was staying at Summerton, together with any of us children who cared to join the party. The usual route was—first to the kennels which were about three-quarters of a mile away, and then home through the fields where my father had a herd of Jersey cattle. The proceedings wound up with an inspection of the garden, which was my mother's domain.

One Sunday, as he came out of the house, something unusual caught my father's eye; this proved to be Arthur, quite a small boy, running along the broad granite parapet which went the whole way round the flat roof of the house.

My father was appalled, and cried "Good Heavens! Look at the child. He'll be killed! Can't you do anything to stop him".

My mother—who was very short-sighted and never used her spectacles except for reading or writing or for other work in the house—peered up at Arthur and said—"I think he'll be alright if you don't distract his attention, but can you see if he has taken off his Sunday clothes?"

As we grew older and were all at home for the holidays, lunch usually found us a big party of all ages, and my father being in Dublin, my mother was in sole control. She ran it rather as if she was the chairman of a public meeting, keeping her eyes and ears open to prevent the outbreak of any argument that might lead to trouble. If one of the party made some verbal attack on another, she said at once, "Now that's enough, I'll have no recriminations!" and so the rising temperature was lowered; but if you bided your time, later on in the proceedings you could get in the necessary retort when the first attack had been forgotten, and before she could stop you. But invariably the "No recrimination" order was immediately repeated.

As I grew on in years I found this a very good training for myself whether as chairman or one of a Committee. If you are quick you can always get in the remark of which you know the chairman will disapprove. You can withdraw it gracefully, amid slight murmurs of appreciation of your action, but you *have* said it. Equally in the chair, if you keep a few seconds ahead, you can often prevent the unwanted remark from being uttered.

My mother read a great deal. She could read, and knit or crochet at the same time, working the needles by her sense of touch and using her eyes entirely for the book. She knitted all our socks and from October onwards was more often than not engaged in crocheting shawls for all the old women in the cottages about the neighbourhood—many of them wives or mothers of my Father's employees. It is the fashion nowadays, particularly in Irish newspapers, to make fun of what they call the "Lady Bountiful" of the old days. My mother would never have claimed to be anything of that sort, but the shawls made to be distributed at Christmas, together with such things as milk puddings and the like, sent to invalids in poor cottages, were always most welcome in days when there was very little public relief beyond the poor house.

114

Of course the reason for the "Lady Bountiful" jokes is, that the ladies who gave this form of assistance were usually wives of landlords—and landlords are fair game. The landlords' case in Ireland went by default, as no one bothered to make it; but taking it all in all, there was much to be said for them, and they did more good in their country than they have ever been given credit for. They were indeed sorely missed in many a neighbourhood, when their helping hand was gone. That could have been amply proved (if anyone ever had taken the trouble to enquire) by investigation among the people who lived round their demesnes, and who were their employees and tenants.

I believe much of the movement from country to city and much of the loss through emigration of valuable young men and women from the Republic is due in some part to the cessation of employment that the big houses, now closed, and still closing all through the country, once gave. With their attendant demesnes, farms, gardens, woods, game preserving, and all the rest, the big houses provided work for the redundant sons and daughters of many a farmer who had not the means of providing for them at home.

While we were still living at Pickering a Nursery Governess, Miss Stubbs, was brought in to continue the education that had been started by my mother. The books used were the same as she had employed—a series published by the educational authorities for use in the National Schools. There were six books in all, and in the schools a boy who worked through all six in the not-very-long-time during which he went to school, was accounted to have done well, as he would also have learned writing and arithmetic.

Boys who were employed at Summerton, not long from school themselves, wishing to find out how our education was progressing, were wont to ask, when greeting us on our return from school for the holidays

"Well what book are ye in now?"

115

There were reading lessons that grew more and more difficult as the student progressed from book to book, and dictation was taken from them. Long lists of words with their meanings had to be learnt by syllables as spelling lessons, such as "BI (bi), SHOP (shop) = BISHOP, a church dignitary", BA (ba), BOON (boon) = BABOON, a large species of ape". We also did poetry, "The Loss of the Royal George", "The Burial of Sir John Moore", and "The Boy stood on the Burning Deck" and such cheery verses had to be learnt by heart.

Augustine had a book of his own, Andrew Lang's "Blue Poetry Book", and he used to recite what he learnt from this standing on the nursery table. The one I particularly remember was:—

> "It was the Schooner Hesper-us
> That sailed the wintry sea
> And the Skipper had taken his little daugh-ter
> To bear him Companee"

And of course there was "Little Arthur's History of England". My mother, whilst encouraging each of us to read books ourselves (as soon as we could do so), always read aloud to us in the winter after tea. The first book I remember is "The Fairchild Family" to which we invented a sequel, unfortunately never written down, in which Mr. Fairchild turned out to be Burglar Bill, and put the spoons and forks into his pockets and any other plate which he could dispose of about his person whenever he went out to dine with his friends.

Writing was taught through the medium of the Vere Foster Copy Books. On the top of each page in copperplate hand were written such ennobling sentiments as "Honesty is the Best Policy", "Never too late to Mend" (this I suppose to redeem the child who had not correctly imbibed the previous one) and the pupil ineffectually struggled to make three

116

copies of each. More often than not the copies became less and less like the original as the child got tired, or fed up.

Arithmetic began with the "Twice one's two", "Twice two's four", and so on with mild sums interspersed.

We learnt the Beatitudes, and also went once a week to the Rectory at Celbridge with other children to receive Bible lessons from Canon Graham. We studied and learnt a psalm[1] some of the verses of which are now considered unsuitable, and accordingly are missed out at many Church of Ireland services. I remember getting my finger nipped in the door of the brougham as we were starting out for the Rectory. A black blister formed very quickly and was exhibited during the lesson for the inspection of those children near enough to enjoy it.

Unexpectedly Miss Stubbs (presumably on instructions from higher authorities) told us that we must not speak the Irish brogue. This was an error of judgement as none of us knew what she was talking about. Admittedly we had long talks with a man called Masterson who had had an accident as a result of which an eye had been removed, and who, on being asked if the removal had been very painful, answered—

"Begob it was. I felt as if I had a swoord in me hat".

We had brought this tragic story into the house and it may well have started the campaign. However, being of an inquisitive nature and not understanding what Miss Stubbs meant, we made enquiries and having found out, soon became very proficient—even learning some dialects other than the local variety and how to imitate different people. With broadminded generosity we passed on all this information to Arthur and Johnnie, and Johnnie became so expert that a nursery maid was once heard saying to him—"Ah Masther Johnnie, don't be talkin' in such a brogue. Anyone'd think ye'd been brought up in the workhouse".

---

[1]Psalm 129 Verses 19-24.

Later on we had a North of Ireland nursery-maid and we learnt that accent too, but we were not so good at it as Geoffrey, my youngest brother. Annie Haddock, as the nursery-maid was called, stayed many years with us and Geoffrey saw more of her than we had done. Having other advantages which we had never been allowed, and usually referred to by my father as "running wild in the stables", Geoffrey attained to a proficiency in different accents and a repertoire that was quite remarkable.

Irish people whether they are conscious of it or not have a certain defined accent, with some it is slight, with others more pronounced, and the Irish are usually quite easily recognised. I met a man, who like myself was walking round the ruins at Ephesus, and after we had been talking for sometime I said, "You and I come from the same country, *Ireland*". He asked me how I knew and I replied "I was fairly sure by your voice, but you confirmed it when I asked you a question and you answered 'It is' instead of 'Yes' ".

He was delighted, saying that he was on his way home after a considerable time in the Far East and considered it very creditable that his nationality could still be so easily recognised. Apart from any accent, the Irish voice is usually softer, more quiet, and has a lower pitch than that of English people when they are speaking their own language.

My brother, Augustine, had other accomplishments as well as his recitations. We had a certain awed respect for him because as quite a small boy he ate and enjoyed marmalade at breakfast, a feat which none of the rest of us could match, and stranger still, he ate mutton fat and enjoyed it—while I turned away from it in horror. He was a most accomplished tease and used to bait me until I lost my temper, which of course gave him great pleasure. Our Nannie described him as a "fagot!"

On one occasion I had had enough and rose up holding

my toy cart in both hands by the shafts—bringing it smartly down on his head. Augustine said he always carried the scar.

There was a real row about that incident and I was sent to bed; I felt however it was thought that there were extenuating circumstances as in due course I was given hot buttered toast for tea, a dish which I had never seen before; but the cart was no longer any good as a cart! When we were both well over forty, someone said to me that she believed I was frightened of Augustine, and I answered—"So would you be if you had travelled two-in-a-pram with him".

When the move was made from Pickering to Summerton, Miss Stubbs retired and was replaced by Miss Dawson. The newcomer was a very bad teacher but a strong walker. After lunch she would take us for walks that were really very long for small boys and one Sunday when I was walking to Church with her (a distance of about two miles) after running breathlessly behind her for about a quarter of a mile, she suddenly picked up her dress on both sides and cried . . . "Now we must put our best foot forward!" At the tender age of seven I knew no expression suitable for the occasion and there was nothing for it but to run faster. The extraordinary thing is that none of us was ever sick in Church.

In addition to the many other things we disliked about Miss Dawson there was the fact that she was an ardent admirer of Gladstone and possessed a chip of wood which she said had been picked at Hawarden in a place where he had been cutting down a tree. She did not hesitate to sing the praises of Gladstone, loudly and often, in a house where Gladstone's name was anathema, not so much because of his attacks on Irish Landlords, but because of the way in which he had despoiled the Church of Ireland.

Not much notice was taken of Miss Dawson's views, and I doubt very much if in the dining-room she had any idea that she was treading on thin ice; but if she had gone into the "gents" (which of course she never did) she would have

119

realised the position, for she would have found in there—in a prominent place, a small piece of bedroom china with an engraved portrait of Gladstone at the bottom. It was one of several made at Belleek especially to the order of a well-known Irishman who had sent them to his friends at Christmas in the way cards are now sent. I only know of three of these and they are all in the possession of people whose name is Brooke.

Miss Dawson only lasted slightly over a year. A change was made as soon as it was realised that in addition to being a bore, she was a very bad teacher.

In our early days at Summerton there was no such thing as a telephone or bicycle, so that a telegram, or an urgent call for the doctor, was sent by a man on a horse, whilst notes to neighbours, or messages of the lesser kind, were taken by those boys whose turn it was for the afternoon ride. Those taking the walk with the governess often took in the post office on the round, and several times while Mrs. Graham attended to the counter we heard in the background the roars and shouts of the telegraph boy who was being beaten by Mr. Graham the postmaster for having dawdled on his round.

Miss Dawson was succeeded by Miss Bliss. This lady was undoubtedly a good teacher, and adding French, Latin and History to the type of learning we had had before, she grounded us well for school. Miss Bliss was really a boys' governess and was much too tough for girls. We all went one by one to school at ten years, well taught in what was required at that age, but my sisters when small, particularly Rosie, had a really bad time with Miss Bliss.

We kept rabbits. They were very smart rabbits—white with black ears, noses and scuts. All were given high-sounding names suitable for the stud book. Johnnie was in charge of them and when he went to school Emily deputised. It is recorded that he wrote to her from school, saying ... "Put Summerton Belle in with Lord Kitchener of Khartoum on the

14th and 15th July so that she may have young the first week of the holidays".

The surplus stock was sold for some minute price to a dealer in rabbits and canaries and such like; he was called King and had a shop in Bride Street, Dublin. When there was a glut in the market and no sale, we made a presentation to the Zoo and inspected with pride a label which stated "Rabbits presented to the Zoo by the Masters Brooke". There seemed to be a high rate of mortality among these rabbits . . . and we had awful suspicions that they were fed to the snakes.

Miss Bliss had a small Dandie Dinmont terrier called 'Sting' which we cordially disliked. For some years, during the last three weeks of the summer holidays we used to go to Larne for the sea and change of air. One year for some reason we went later than usual and found to our distress that Miss Bliss was also coming. There were to be lessons—and of course Sting was brought along. After lessons one day we reported to Miss Bliss, with feelings of nervous pleasure, that Sting was walking about in front of the house with about a yard of string hanging from his mouth, and that he was trying to bite it off, but in the attempt was gradually swallowing it. Miss Bliss forthwith charged at Sting, seized the string and pulled—when out came more string. This went on until she had raised quite a sizeable heap of the stuff. Then the string stuck . . . Miss Bliss gave a good jerk, Sting was sick immediately and a filthy piece of mutton fat shot out, tied to the end of the string. Miss Bliss and Sting were both much relieved, but Arthur was furious claiming that this was his bait and line for catching crabs and that now he would have to start all over again.

Emily, who was in Miss Bliss's care until she was fourteen, took her measure, and having a much quicker tongue, gradually defeated her. One day a dish was handed to Miss Bliss with only two portions left in it, one much bigger than the

121

other. Miss Bliss took the larger one (though it was alleged that the smaller was nearer to her) leaving the other for Geoffrey. To everyone's surprise at her unwonted generosity, Emily rushed round the table and shovelled most of her portion on to Geoffrey's plate, saying that she could not think of allowing him to be put off with such a miserable helping. Miss Bliss lost her head and said she had not noticed any difference in the size of the helpings. Of course my mother was not present. A few days later when again she was absent, Emily had the cream jug balanced in her hand, trying to get the blob on to her plate, and Miss Bliss called anxiously, "Remember, Emily, there are others besides yourself" . . . To which Emily retorted, "Well! who took the biggest helping the other day?"

These scenes were described to my mother who decided that Miss Bliss had lost her touch and could no longer enforce discipline and that a change must be made. Emily had completely broken Miss Bliss's spirit—indeed she said she could not be a governess any longer; a place was therefore found for her as companion to an invalid lady (who was related to Mrs. B.) in the North of Ireland.

As mentioned before, at the age of ten years, we were all sent off to a preparatory school, primarily in my father's view to get rid of such brogues as we had in permanent use, while my mother, approving of course of this desirable object, was really more interested in the cause of education.

We went to a school at Laleham on the Thames kept by Frank Buckland, a famous cricketer. He had been at Eton with Uncle Gerald whose sons, Dick and Gougs, were the first Brookes to go to Laleham, in 1890. From that time until 1906 a procession of Brookes passed through the school, seven of us and four cousins.

It was a school with a certain amount of tradition, having been founded in 1821 by Thomas Arnold of Rugby, and his brother-in-law, John Buckland (Frank Buckland's grand-father[1]). They had bought a large house near the village of Laleham described as "a delightful spot, leafy and luxurious on the North Side of the Thames . . . in those times the village was small and exclusive the river quiet and safe for bathing".

It was exactly the same when I went there in 1895 and we bathed in the summer and were taught to swim. Thomas Arnold and John Buckland kept the school in partnership until 1824 when they agreed to set up separate establishments. Buckland kept the big house and Arnold moved into a smaller one nearby where he took older boys preparing for the University, a house into which Frank Buckland's mother moved after his marriage. When John Buckland died, his son Mathew took over the school. He had the same views on small boys and corporal punishment as are credited to his Uncle Thomas Arnold. There were several members of Kildare Street Club rather younger than my father who had been there and who used to tell me about their experiences in the school. One of them told me that Mathew Buckland rejoiced in rapping a small boy hard on the knuckles with a ruler on a frosty morning. One of the others who had been listening broke in, "Don't you remember how, when he died, the boys broke out of the school, lined the wall the other side of the road, and cheered when the coffin was brought out?"

Frank Buckland succeeded his father, and whilst not dis-approving of corporal punishment, he employed it sparingly, three or four canings a term being the average, and usually the victims were boys who had been operated on before. Towards the end of my time at Laleham, Frank substituted an old fashioned long-handled fives bat for the cane. *I* never required such treatment but one of the boys who had suffered several times told me that the fives bat did not hurt as much as the cane but was more alarming owing to the terrific

[1]*Thomas Arnold.* T. W. Bamford, Cresset Press 1960.

123

bang it made at the moment of impact. We were all fond of Frank and had a very deep respect for him.

Of course we played football in the winter and cricket in summer, as I did afterwards at Winchester, but only for two summers did I play cricket, for I disliked the game.

When the end of term came, we Irish boys (as was the case in all properly conducted schools) left for home the night before the other boys. We started off at five o'clock, and if Aunt Rose was in London she provided us with sausages and mash in her studio in Yeoman's Row, and when she was not there we had a meal at the Euston Hotel. Crossings in the winter were usually dreadful! In my first years of crossing we travelled in the old paddle boats, then after two years the new twin screw steamers were put on, which considerably shortened the time taken for the crossing. We usually arrived at Summerton about 8 a.m. and I never remember the boat being late at Kingstown owing to bad weather, although this must have happened.

During the Christmas holidays we realised the great advantage of being the sons of a wine merchant, as the magnificent Christmas presents from the shippers abroad began to arrive. Barton and Guestier at Bordeaux sent large white porcelain terrines of Perigord Pie and boxes of nougat. From Oporto, Sandeman and Cockburn sent boxes of preserved fruits, on the top layers of which were pinned little bows and rosettes of silver wire and small coloured artificial flowers which helped to make a very pretty dish for dessert; and Sandeman Buck & Co. sent Spanish hams from Xerez. Two Champagne houses, Pol Roger and Perrier Jouet, sent enormous Strasbourg Pies, pastry filled with pâté de foie gras, and boxes of champagne biscuits known as "Tarpin". There were other gifts, also, and as a Director of the Bank of Ireland, my father received a small sack of perfect apples which were known as the "Bank Apples". A certain man who once owed money to the Bank, and had been leniently treated, had gone out to British Columbia where he had prospered as a fruit farmer. In appreciation of his excellent treatment by the Bank he sent one of these small bags of his own, very high-class apples to each of the Directors of the Bank, and to the Secretary and the Accountant General.

All the presents from the shippers became casualties of the 1914-18 War and did not appear again with peace—but the apples continued! One year I recall the Bank apples coming to table for dessert and not re-appearing. My father asked where they were, and Kynes with a broad grin said that by mistake they had been used for cooking. Then there was a real blow up! Kynes hurriedly changed his cheerful expression to one of sorrow, but it was too late, and the vials of my father's wrath were emptied on his head, to be repeated in the proper quarters downstairs. Probably the only result below stairs was an extra glass of port all round. Kynes used to indent at fairly frequent intervals for what he called "Lunshon" port. It never appeared in the dining-room and it was well-known where it went, but no comment was made, as Kynes alleged that some doctor had ordered him to have a daily glass of port.

All this sounds very greedy but we had made strict rules of the game which were always observed. For instance, you might make only one plunge with the scoop into the Perigord or Strasbourg Pie and you took out what you had collected but could not go back for more. In the pies there were fine truffles, one of which—or even part of one—when captured would be considered a great prize. You might not probe or search for a truffle—but if you saw even a sign of one you could plunge in the scoop, and get out the truffle with as much of the *foie gras* as you could. If you cut the truffle in half, the second half had to be left, fair game for the next candidate. So the thing was, to keep an eye on the pie and if possible mark down a truffle while the pie was still a place or two off, and hope that those on your right might not notice it.

9

Geoffrey, when about six years old, had on one occasion marked down a truffle and when the time came, firmly wrenched it out with some *pâté* as well. On his left was an uncle, a great gourmet, who was heard murmuring to himself— "Look at that child. He has about three guineas' worth on his plate and he doesn't appreciate it in the least".

This was not correct. While we had no idea of its monetary value, we all of us fully appreciated the *foie gras* as very desirable food. It was there, and it reappeared each Christmas, and we never realised that ordinarily it was an expensive luxury. We took it for granted and accepted it as it came along—just as we did many more important things that went to make up our happiness in those halcyon days.

There were always enough boys' mounts to allow two or even three brothers to go out hunting on the same day during the Christmas holidays, most frequently with my father's own harriers, but also in Meath or Kildare when they were attended by Shepherd, who was a most remarkable character. He supervised the youth whose job it was to boil the porridge for the hounds, and he carried out the other and more grizzly duties that had to be performed. While Shepherd was not kennel huntsman, he was in fact huntsman, and hunted hounds when my father was not out. He was not groom, but he superintended the stables so far as the hunters were concerned. He was actually called the Steward and he looked after everything that had to do with the farm. Shepherd saw to it that the boy who drove the pony in the pump did his work properly and that the big water tank in the stable-yard (which was the day-to-day reservoir that supplied the house, stableyard and garden) was kept filled and he looked after the out-of-doors end of the sanitary arrangements and the drains. His wife managed the dairy, making first-class butter: also cream cheeses. She was Scottish. Shepherd was a York-shireman, his father having been a tenant on Sir Tatton Sykes' estate. My father said he was one of a small number of men with whom he had to deal during his life who were absolutely and completely honest and whom he could trust implicitly; and this not only as regards what he had in his own hands, but because he would always tell my father of anything dubious about which he thought my father ought to know. He came one day to my father, saying "You'd better get rid of yon butler". My father asked him what he meant . . . "Well, he's carrying on with cook and if you don't get rid of him there'll be trouble in the house".

My father said, "I can't get rid of him just like that! I have no proof of anything and I would lay myself open to an action for slander by both him and the cook. What proof have you? How do you know?", and Shepherd said, "Wot if butler forgot to pull down blind?".

So the butler went, and not long afterwards the cook gave notice. No one minded about the butler, but the cook had been first-class at her job.

Arthur had for a long time borne a particular grudge against this butler. He had handed his plate to the footman one day saying he wanted a second helping. And he heard the footman say, "Master Arthur wants a second helping". To which the butler replied . . . "Master Arthur can wait!" Master Arthur, about six years old, got down from his chair, went round the screen and delivered a most frightful punch into the butler's stomach which doubled him up, the young gentleman saying at the same time—"That'll teach you to say I can wait for my second helping".

Of course there was a row, Arthur was sent out of the room and later was taken to the butler to apologise. All this he obediently did, but it was quite obvious that he did not mean what he said.

There is no doubt that of all the many duties undertaken by Shepherd, that of looking after Francis, Augustine and Arthur when out hunting, was the one he most thoroughly enjoyed, as *they* did. He gave them a lead so that they saw a great deal, and as he knew exactly what their ponies could do, there was never any risk of their getting into trouble. "Trivy" who reported for "The Field" recorded what a pleasure it was to see Mr. George Brooke's sons out "Shepherded by their father's huntsman." Shepherd's hunting coats and waistcoats, the ones he wore on this job as well as the green coat that he wore with the Harriers, were made by the firm of Robinson & Steele, the kings of Dublin tailors, and years afterwards they told Arthur that Shepherd was one of their most exacting clients, and that there was always a great deal of trouble before Mr. Shepherd was finally satisfied.

Being a very large family of varying ages (a half-brother born in 1877 and seven brothers and two sisters born between 1882 and 1896) we really were self-contained and supplied for ourselves all the amusements and society we wanted without going outside. In addition to the hunting in the winter there was light diversion in the way of sport provided by about four couple of very small beagles, which were used in the off seasons for hunting rabbits. There were not many rabbits and the stock was not reduced as much as anyone would notice by the beagles. They were all in two ditches in one field, and the burrows were carefully stopped, but the rabbits usually had the best of it.

When in the Christmas holidays my mother announced that she had accepted an invitation to go to a party there were always groans which went on continuously until the day of the affair arrived. My mother, however, would take no notice of these demonstrations, except to say on the day of the party— "You know quite well you'll enjoy yourselves when you get there", and in this she was as usual quite correct.

On the way to and from school, if she happened to be in London, we always spent the day or as much of it as there was, with Aunt Rose. The Aquarium and Madam Tussaud's were the two great indoor standbys. At Madam Tussaud's the great thing was to get one of the party to go and buy a programme from one of the wax figures of programme sellers which were carefully ranged about and this was quite often brought off. At the Aquarium, the performing fleas were a great attraction. To our delight there was one harnessed into an outside car. When not on show they were stabled on cotton wool and the owner fed them on his own arm. It was said that Queen Victoria commanded that they should be brought to Windsor to give their performance before her. At the end of the show she expressed herself much pleased. When the owner was packing up, he found to his dismay that one flea was missing! He was much distressed as he said it was his best flea. The Queen was very sympathetic and the Ladies-in-Waiting joined in the search for the flea, which was eventually found on Queen Victoria. It was duly handed back to the owner who said it was a beautiful flea—but not the one he had lost!

Outdoor amusements were the Tower and the Zoo. At the Zoo there was a monkey which for some reason detested women and there was a notice on the cage to the effect that he was on no account to be annoyed. On one particular visit one of us "kept cave" while Aunt Rose stood in front of the cage and opened her umbrella, whereupon the monkey flew into a rage, made balls of the sawdust in his cage and hurled them at her. She was in those days, as indeed to the end of her life, the most delightful companion. I think she enjoyed these outings, but she must have been dead-beat by the time we departed for home or for school.

On one occasion things went badly. Arthur and Johnnie, who for some reason had come up from Laleham earlier in the day than usual, delightedly agreed to her suggestion that, it being a very hot day, they should all go out in a boat on the pond in St. James' Park. They embarked in charge of a boatman and soon Arthur and Johnnie began to rock the boat. The boatman of course got very angry and said they would all be upset into the water—which caused roars of laughter.

Then Aunt Rose also got angry! She had no fears of being drowned, but she had no wish to come up on shore through a London crowd with two boys and herself all drenched to the skin, and then have to seek some means of getting the boys home and dried so that they might get away on the Irish Mail. So she told the boatman to land them and they disembarked.

Arthur had both bootlaces undone, Johnnie had a stocking down round his ankle, Aunt Rose was hot and dishevelled and had lost a glove. At that time, being gloveless in public in London was, for a lady, almost on a par with being half naked. She then realised that approaching her, on his way home from the Horse Guards, looking dapper as if he had just stepped out of a band box, and holding out his hand, was Lord Wolseley whom she had known well when he was Commander of the Forces in Ireland. She felt that her cup was full, but there was nothing for it but to stand her ground.

*   *   *

Heus! Rogere, fer caballos
Eja, nunc eamus;
Limen Amabile,
Matris et oscula
Suaviter et repetamus.
Domum, Domum, dulce Domum . . . .

8. *Swansong at Summerton*

FROM Laleham we all went in turn to Winchester with
the exception of Johnnie who went to the Britannia. He
was the first of the family to pass an examination for the
Britannia, Woolwich, or Sandhurst at first try. Augustine
had passed into Sandhurst at his second, through a crammer,
while Arthur achieved Woolwich from Winchester at his
first attempt—but this was later. Francis had got a Commission
in the 60th Rifles from Militia Service in the South African
War but the cousins and my half-brother, none of them caring
much, had failed repeatedly.

When the time drew near for the Britannia list to be published, my mother had the morning paper sent to her room as
soon as it arrived. On the day the list appeared she began,
from bitter experience, to read the list from the bottom up; she
read on and on, her heart sinking, fearing yet another disap-
pointment—and then she found John Brooke right at the top

among the single figures! She sent the paper to him at once
with instructions that as she was going to be late, he must
read prayers in her place. This he did with great dignity, but
we of his congregation, who had not passed an examination
and were hungry for breakfast, began to wonder when he
was going to stop.

The rest of us went to Trant Bramston's House at Winchester where we had satisfactory but undistinguished careers.

Our family was really divided into two sections—five boys
in the older one, two boys and a girl in the younger, with
Emily in between. Johnnie, the youngest in the older section,
was seven years senior to Basil, the eldest of the younger one,
so as we passed through Winchester, the younger lot were
getting ready for Laleham. In the holidays many amusements
were arranged in an informal way, most of them more or
less suitable to all of us. My father came home from Dublin
one day rather earlier than usual, and walked out to see what
was going on. He walked past the house, and was hidden
from view by a large yew bush, when there crossed his path,
coming from the direction of the stables—one of his pigs—
much out of breath but still gallantly cantering. It ran on a
short way and then lay down in the middle of a large and
well-stocked flower-bed. Before my father had time to move
there was a good deal of hilarious shouting, then George and
Arthur appeared on bicycles following the line of the pig—
each armed with a billiard cue, one tipped with white chalk,
the other with green; Alas! with authority standing behind
the yew bush, they had no opportunity of deciding who got
the first spear.

At the other end of the scale (nine years younger than
Johnnie) was Geoffrey, who, when he was quite a small boy
had a donkey called "Old Doyle". Old Doyle was groomed
and looked after entirely by Geoffrey so that he was very
smartly turned out, and furthermore he was fed on the best
oats so that he was quite fit and for a donkey was quite a good

jumper. Being an intelligent donkey he soon realised that it was wisest to jump any fence his owner put him at. As a result of all this, Geoffrey was usually fairly grubby save when he had been caught and cleaned up for meals. One fine day a general and his wife—both very smart, arrived unexpectedly for tea, bringing with them their son who was about the same age as Geoffrey. This child was quite beautifully dressed in a long box-cloth coat, with very large buttons, and a hat of the same calibre—all reminiscent of the Brighton Road. My mother took one look at him and decided that this was not a suitable playmate for Geoffrey. There was no knowing what the Regency Buck might look like at the end of the day when Geoffrey had finished with him, so she said she did not know where Geoffrey was. When the time came for the guests to depart, the General went out to the stables with my father to fetch his dogcart and the child went too. On the way, much to my father's dismay, they met Geoffrey making his way in to tea and looking quite as grubby as had been feared. Geoffrey however sized up the situation quite accurately, held to his course—and as they passed he touched his cap to my father, saying in his best brogue, "Fine day, Sir Garge!" My father returned the salute, but otherwise ignored his son and the situation was saved. When my mother was told the story she was rather hurt that her youngest offspring should have been cut by his father, but at the same time she realised that she could not have it both ways.

A certain Captain Pryce who often came for week-ends told my mother that when staying recently in another house in the neighbourhood he had met Geoffrey riding Old Doyle. "And I'm sorry to have to say it, but he was *very* dirty". My mother at once defended her son and said . . . "Oh no! Captain Pryce, I'm sure he was not as bad as all *that*", but the Captain refused to withdraw and said . . . "Oh yes! . . . You know how fond I am of your boys and how I'd stand up for them anywhere, but he *was* dirty, he was *filthy*. You could hardly tell him from the ground".

Jack Pryce, as he was called, was very fat and short. Someone who knew him in his young days told us that when he joined the 13th Hussars, he was the neatest looking little figure imaginable. The first time our informant saw him was at a circus run by the 13th Hussars in India when he cantered into the ring standing on one horse and driving three in front of him. When I knew Captain Pryce he was almost a double cube! He suffered a lot from gout which he said was hereditary but I always felt he had earned every twinge. He had a charming place in Wales but his wife, whom he had married late in life and who was a good deal younger than he, refused to live there, and as she was Irish, they came to live at Ballybrack (which he called Ballyjack) near Dublin.

The seat of his trousers was always ten inches below where the tailor intended it to be, and when he walked in front of you, the back view was like the hind legs of an elephant. A doctor having told him that a little gentle exercise would be good, he bought a tricycle. He had a servant called Mark, and when they came to stay at Summerton, a hack cab met them at Westland Row Station, in Dublin; Mark extracted the Captain's baggage from the train and it and the Captain were put into the cab, and the procession started, Mark riding behind on the tricycle. Mark pedalled all through Dublin and up the steep slope of the Phoenix Park as far as the Phoenix Monument. There, unless the wind was against them, in which case he rode the whole way, Mark got into the cab and the Captain rode the tricycle slowly as far as the exit from the Park at White's Gate. The slope being against him he got back into the cab and finished the journey inside. In the distance it was not always easy to tell which was which —until you realised that Mark wore a bowler hat and the Captain an enormous check cap.

When in good form Jack Pryce could be very amusing.

One night after dinner he announced that he was going to sing (quite a new venture), the audience being my father and mother and myself. The Captain stood up in the middle of the room and said he had put the song together himself from well-known ditties of his young days and he begged that it might not be written down as he did not wish anyone to sing it but himself. Then he began and sang with much feeling—

> "Why was I born so beautiful?
>   The girls all call me jam
>   I might have been lean, ugly, fat
>   Instead of what I am" . . . .

. . . then at greatly increased speed and singing fortissimo, he bawled;—

> "Has anyone seen my Mary Anne?
>   She kicked up 'er 'eels and away she ran
>   We tried to stop 'er as 'ard as we could
>   But she wanted to go and go she would
>   She'd a kind friend in London to give her a start
>   And now she's become a Society Tart"

piano and slower—

> "Aow! Aow! the ship is rollin' hover
>   Aow! Capting 'ow far is it to Dover?"
>   etc. etc.

Now pastry was not a frequent topic of conversation in the drawing-room at Summerton—and when it was mentioned, it was the kind used in making mince pies and so forth. Uncertain as to how my father and mother might take this outburst of the Captain's, I thought it wise to wait and see. My mother stood up to it well, and when I looked at my father I saw tears of mirth pouring down his cheeks. I felt then that I too could give way to my emotion.

Seeing that he had got it across so well the Captain started off on what he considered to be the best things in his repertoire of stories. They were mostly of Welsh origin and recounted in a strong Welsh accent. He told of a certain important magnate in Wales, quite young, who was uncouth in appearance and manners, and whose family prevailed on him that it would be greatly to his advantage if he were to obtain a Commission in the Army. When he made his request at the War Office, the clerk suggested a Commission in a Line Regiment.

"Well, no. I wanted a Commission in a Cavalry Regiment and I would prefer the Life Guards or the Blues".

"But you know, Sir, you would require a considerable income to live in those regiments".

"Well, I have twenty-five thousand a year now, and when my mother do die, which please God will be shortly, I shall have twelve thousand a year more, and I suppose I could scrat along on that".

Then we got going on the Merionethshire Yeomanry of which the Captain's father had been Colonel. There had been a great deal of continual talking and noise in the ranks which the Colonel said must stop! On one occasion there was noise almost like a fight, and an aggrieved man on being told off, said,

"Well. What it is is, I, Hugh Lloyd, ride small pony, on my right is John Jones, on big horse, and the rowel of his spur is always in my knee".

Then the great day came when the Regiment was to be inspected by Lord Cardigan—and almost under pain of death they were told that the chatter *must* cease. Then the Captain went on, "They were all lined up on the Parade Ground, when Cardigan, who liked doing something dramatic, came up at full gallop, slung jacket flying, sabretache and all that, and a glittering staff following him. He pulled up his horse on its haunches, gravel and dust flying in every direction. There was dead silence—and then came an anguished cry from the ranks . . . "Gracious God! Edward Morgan, what a livery he has got!"

Another story was of the private soldier who told the sergeant that he was ill and on being asked what was the matter with him said he had a pain in his bowels. "Bowels" said the sergeant, "You ain't got bowels. It's only orficers as 'as bowels. You've got guts." Nowadays people are U or non-U. We divided the community up into "bowels" or "guts".

Finally came the one we got to know as "The Leith Bottle Cart". The 13th were quartered in or near Edinburgh and a brother officer took Jack for a drive in his dogcart. They had an unfortunate collision with what Jack described as a Leith Bottle Cart. The horse in the cart was knocked down, the bottles were broken in every direction and the horse was so cut that it had to be destroyed. The owner of the bottle cart took an action for damages, and Jack Pryce had to give evidence on behalf of his friend. The opposing lawyer opened his cross-examination by reminding Jack in a loud and threatening voice that he was on his oath. Jack said sweetly, "Oh, yes! I understand that".

"Well, Mr. Pryce, on your oath now . . . "

"Yes, I said I understood that".

"Well, on your oath, was there another man in the bottle cart?"

"No".

(With a loud roar) . . . "On your oath now, Mr. Pryce, was there or was there not another man in the bottle cart?"

"If there was—he was under the bottles!"

Pryce played a lot of bridge in Kildare Street Club. He was a very bad player and I once heard his unfortunate partner, a man from Galway, with a magnificent brogue, say—

"It's you to play, Pryce".

"Yes, I know . . . I'm thinking".

"Well, I wish you wouldn't think—because I obsairve that whenever you think, I lose half-a-crown".

Jack Pryce was very rich and he was very fond of one of my younger brothers whom he called the "young Guvnor". When the "Young Guvnor" married, we were all rather disappointed that the cheque from the Captain amounted to no more than £5. About ten years later, on his death, he was stated to have had £100,000 in his current account.

My father and mother were extremely hospitable, and genuinely enjoyed entertaining their friends. There were always two or three to lunch on Sundays, who in summer usually spent the afternoon at Summerton and went away after dinner. There were friends of all ages; soldiers and their wives who were quartered in Dublin and about whom we had heard from friends in England, young soldiers in the same category and others who had been at school with us. Visitors to the house came and went in an unending stream, and of course there were many relations (and sons of relations) from England and Scotland, and indeed even from Australia —Barton relations of my mother. It was a rule of the house, that if it could be prevented, no one bearing the name Brooke left Ireland without staying for a few days at Summerton. Basil Brooke, afterwards Admiral, and Controller and Equerry to King George VI, when Duke of York, told me that when about twenty-six, he met my father for the first time, and mentioned that he hoped shortly to go to Ireland on a visit to Colebrooke. My father said, "You can't do that without coming to see us at Summerton, either on your way to Colebrooke or going back. You'll have no difficulty in finding the house. You can smell the roast beef at the lodge gates and there won't be change for half-a-crown in the house".

Occasionally there were old friends of my father's from his Eton or Cambridge days. One turned up quite unexpectedly on a certain occasion, whom my father had not heard of for

years, and indeed who he thought had in fact been certified
and shut up in an asylum. However he came to see my father in
Dublin and was asked out to lunch on the following Sunday.
A short time afterwards a complete stranger appeared and
informed my father that his friend had escaped from a private
lunatic asylum, that he himself was a keeper who had been
sent after him, and that the patient (though quite harmless)
had to be brought back. On the following Sunday the old
school friend turned up at Summerton on an outside car
accompanied by the keeper, having agreed that he would
go back quietly to the asylum if he was allowed to lunch at
Summerton. Lunch that day was a splendid entertainment.
The visitor got hold of a soda water syphon which unfortunately got the better of him when he tried to put what he
wanted into his tumbler, and everyone within range was
drenched. He had been put sitting next to my mother, at her
end of the table, when he suddenly called out to my father at
the other end:—

"George, did you know my father-in-law?"

"No, I don't think I did".

"My father-in-law nicest ol' boy you ever met. My mother-
in-law biggest ol' bitch in England".

There was always a full house for the Horse Show, the
core of the party being old friends and contemporaries of my
father, with some a good deal older. Three of those who usually
came had served in the Crimean War, and one of them, Sir
William Gordon of Earlston, who had been in the 17th Lancers,
had ridden in the Charge of the Light Brigade and afterwards
served through the Indian Mutiny. He was badly wounded
in the Charge, a sabre cut having gone deep into the back of
his neck, the scar of which we were allowed to inspect. He
sometimes bought a horse at the Show—it had to be a young
horse and a chestnut. Sir William never brought a man with
him and used to take the horse to the Glasgow boat himself,
put the animal aboard and travel over with him.

The servants at Summerton stayed for years, the younger ones only leaving to get married—the older ones died in service. Annie Haddock, who has figured in this story already, came from the North of Ireland in 1890 as a nursery-maid, then succeeded to the position of Nannie, and finally was my mother's maid. She only left us at the end in 1911, a few months after my mother's death. Annie married Greenham who had been a journeyman in the garden. He served in the 1914–18 war and was taken prisoner in March 1918. On coming home he had started a market garden but died quite unexpectedly. Annie was living in Brighton when war broke out in 1939 and my sister, Emily Persse, persuaded her to come and live at Chattis Hill with her, thinking that Brighton was not going to be a very comfortable place. Annie stayed there till Emily died in 1953. The last time I was there I went to see Annie who was getting rather senile. After some talk I went out and she seized Emily by the arm and said, "Tell me, Duck, who was that?" Emily said, "You know perfectly well, Annie, that was Mr. Raymond". Annie said, "Well, I never. I wouldn't have known a bit of him. He's grown so!" . . . I was then 67 and although it was sixty-two years since Annie had come to us, (and in that time she had hardly ever been back to her home) she had never lost her magnificent North of Ireland accent.

Kynes succeeded as butler "the man who forgot to pull down the blind". He had been with my father at Pickering for about three years and went away to set up a shop in Belfast. This proved a failure and he returned and was with us up to 1911. Kynes was Irish but talked as if he had never been out of England. He was small in stature and told us that he had started life in a racing stable in Co. Waterford, and had then gone to England where he was "second 'orseman to the Markis of Bath"; that while he was there one of his duties was to sit in the rumble at the back of the carriage carrying a blunderbuss, when his Lordship drove to London. We were a little doubtful of the truth of this statement but as it made good copy it was accepted. He was probably very old when he left us but certainly lived in retirement for some eight or nine years afterwards. He was getting rather bothered as the years advanced, and one Sunday on coming in after breakfast with the usual statement, "Brennan is in for orders", he added "and if you please he says Wensleydale is lame". When he went out of the room my father said, "What on earth does he mean? I never had a horse called Wensleydale in my life". Arthur decided that it was the name of Kynes' charger at Waterloo.

Brennan was the coachman. He was born in County Kildare and had been employed from boyhood by Lord Clonmell (Earlie) after whose death he came to Summerton. Brennan was old and ailing when he left us. In fact he only lived two or three weeks longer. The day before he retired he gave my mother a beautiful carriage-whip and said "That is for the young gentlemen". He told her that on leaving Bishopscourt, Lord Clonmell having died, he had been given this whip as a memento. He himself had chosen the hollystick in the rough at Swain & Adeney's and the whip had a silver band with Lord Clonmell's crest and coronet on it.

But as the years went by the machinery was gradually grinding to a standstill! The expensive first-class education provided for all of us, the non-profitable manner in which the farm at Summerton itself, as well as an outlying one in Kildare, had been run—almost entirely to provide oats for hunters, and beef and mutton of the most expensive kind to feed eight hungry sons—all this was gradually taking toll. Nothing was ever sold from the farm, everything went into the house, the stables or the kennels, and the weekly wages bill had always to be met. Finally in November 1910 the crisis came—and we were out of Summerton by the following February. It was sold a few months later. My mother had died in the previous September—so she was spared all this.

The wheel had gone full circle when my father returned to the Governor's original home, 1 Gardiner Row, over the shop. This was to be his headquarters for the next ten years. Then, with the Treaty obviously coming, bringing with it the departure of the British Army (whose Officers' Messes were among our best customers) and also of many other good Irish customers, we wound up while the going was still fairly good.

Francis and his wife[1] had been renting Pickering for some time and my father and sister Rosie went to live with them. He was very happy there, and died in 1926.

---

[1]Mabel, daughter of Sir John Arnott, Bt.

9. *Arthur; 1886-1954*

AS will have been realised the general atmosphere at Summerton, and before that at Pickering, was one of hounds, hunting and riding generally. I never fitted into this. To be strictly truthful I was terrified of riding, and as a child at Pickering when I made my way through the door into the kennel green, the smell overpowered me and I was always sick. Naturally I was encouraged to remain outside. Once a well meaning relation who was staying at Pickering found me standing outside and "took pity on me", opening the door and taking me inside. I was promptly sick, and in the excitement a couple and a half of young hounds escaped through the door which my relation was considerately holding open.

The only ride that as a small child and even later I can remember with pleasure, was on a pony called 'Mons Meg' which George had outgrown. 'Mons Meg' was fat and very old, and fixed tight to the saddle was a small basket-work arm chair with a cushion in it. Into this I was strapped. Somebody led 'Mons Meg' and the feeling of comfort, safety, and confidence, was delightful.

The only instruction I can remember receiving was a rhyme taught me by my Mother,

> "Your head and your heart keep up,
> Your hands and your heels keep down,
> Your knees keep close to your horse's side,
> And your elbows close to your own."

Later we had an Iceland pony called "Piebald" ridden by Francis (and in my opinion a real brute) and also a small Shetland called "Dolly," usually ridden by Augustine and talked of by Shepherd as "Master Gustine's mare". She was nappy but Francis could control the one and Augustine the other while both animals did what they liked with me. Looking back I fancy they had been teased badly by stable boys.

When I was about nine years old I announced that I would ride no more. To make this announcement required as a matter of fact more courage than riding the ponies. Francis and Augustine looked on it as backsliding of the most dreadful kind, and when they went back to school and met Aunt Rose in London, the first words they uttered were—"Have you heard? Raymond's given up riding." Aunt Rose was relieved that it was nothing worse—as from the way the question was put and the expression on their faces, she thought something really bad had happened. My father took the decision quietly, realising that this made one less to mount, and that one likely to be the heavy-weight of the family. I took no more horse exercise until I was forty-seven years old when I was induced by Nigel Bruce of the Imperial Tobacco Company to come out on a hireling in the Phoenix Park. Encouraged by this—

for three seasons on Saturdays I followed the chase in Kildare at a respectful distance, Francis being Joint Master at the time. Then one day I got several falls and was considerably hurt and very indignant, and the same thing happened the following Saturday. By that time I knew too much and realising the dangers involved I decided that the family escutcheon was now wiped clean and that I might stop riding. On that last day when I fell, my hireling to my great relief galloped off into the country and I made for my car, which I had left not very far off. Then an officious man appeared leading the horse and I had to remount—and, what was worse, give him half a crown. That evening Nigel, who had been out with the Ward, rang up my rooms to know if I was back and the servant said, "He's in the bath and he's mud and blood from head to foot."

I always fell heavy and I suppose more so as I got older. Shepherd once told my Father that I had had a fall and was asked if I was hurt. Shepherd said "No, he just fell on his boonkey. Master Raymond falls like any stone." Needless to say this, to us, new word found its way into the nursery vocabulary.

We, none of us, cared much about organised games in the holidays. There really was not room for them and I in particular disliked cricket; therefore it was with feelings rather of dismay that Arthur and I at Winchester received a letter from my mother saying that some boys, known to us only by name, had started a boys' cricket club to play in the holidays. She had entered us as members, and (which made things worse) the blazer which they wished us to get was the same as that worn by Lords at Winchester. However, by the time we arrived home we had forgotten all about the matter until one evening, having been out all day, I was informed that a telegram had come asking for one of us to play the next day and that the invitation had been accepted for me. I felt it most unfair as my mother had put my name in simply because she knew that I was more easily coerced than Arthur, and she feared

145

he might stick in his toes and refuse to go. So off I went, and had a perfectly ghastly day—but as we were never asked to play again, I felt that from our point of view I had done all that was possible.

The game I really enjoyed was golf, and I played a great deal of it at one time when I was working in Dublin. I started when at Winchester, where we had a very sporting small nine-hole course on each side of the Southampton road. Golf was a cheap game in those days, an iron club costing 4/6 and a wooden one 5/6. We played with a gutty ball and the wooden clubs had a piece of leather let into the face to protect it. I still think I got more satisfaction out of a well hit drive with a gutty ball than I ever did with a rubber one. You felt as if you really had hit something. The ball most generally used was the Silvertown and later there was also the Ocobo, either of which cost 1/– and if you were impecunious (a state I was always in) you paid ninepence and got a "remade". Who "remade" them, or how or where, we were never told. In Bramston's House we almost all of us played golf, and his son Johnnie was a very good player who would have gone a long way in the game if he had not died young of consumption. The year after he left Winchester he got into the semi-finals of the Amateur Championship. We had House Foursomes and in these at my first effort I was partnered in the draw with Johnnie Bramston, which was rather an alarming honour. It was a good draw for him because, while his handicap was plus four, mine was thirty, so other pairs in many cases had to give us strokes. On the tee of a short hole when he was to drive he said to me, "We've been playing with my ball so far: it's time you put one down." So I put my remade down and he took his cleek, played a perfect shot and the ball broke in two pieces. Johnnie took it wonderfully well and indeed saw the humour of it. Then there was a discussion as to what you did when the ball broke into two pieces, and it was finally decided that you dropped another as near as you could to the biggest piece, without losing distance. This I did—and was instructed to hit at the ball and miss it. By this time I was trembling all over and made a swipe at the ball and almost hit it. Then Johnnie laid it right against the pin and we won the hole in four. We won the foursomes in the end.

*   *   *   *

Of all my brothers, Arthur was the nearest one to me. He was a little more than a year younger, but we had been two years together at Laleham, and two years at Winchester, the only members of the family at both places during those years, and when I was working in Dublin and he was at Woolwich, we were the only grown-up ones in the home countries. The others were scattered abroad in the Navy and the Army. Therefore more by chance than anything else we were brought more closely together. We grew to know each other very well, discussed our problems, which were always more or less to do with the same subject—finance—and when Arthur went to India in 1908 we corresponded regularly. He always showed the same carefree abandon about his personal safety as he did on the day he was seen running round the parapet of the roof at Summerton, but I shall never forget it to him that when late in life I started to ride, he presented me with a small red book issued by the War Office, marked as well as I remember "Strictly Confidential", which told me everything I must do when riding and all about horse management. Arthur always gave me the idea that he did not mind if he broke his neck, but he was not going to let me break mine. Not that there was any danger, I was much too careful.

He won the Benson prize and the saddle at "The Shop" and was posted to a Battery in India in January 1908. Since he never had much money, it is astonishing how much he did, and how much he saw. He certainly never had anything beyond his pay after the first three years in India.

The sport Arthur most enjoyed was pigsticking, and it was said that in the India of his day he had few equals.

In the records of the Meerut Tent Club for 1911 the early entries begin cheerfully on the 2nd February:—

"Finally Wardrop and Brooke going Southwest and Northeast respectively collided; Brooke's fluent and instantaneous flow of coarse language silenced Wardrop at once. The latter not what he used to be since sad accident to his tongue last year."

and on 4th February:—

"Brooke—sans giglamps—held this boar at his spear's point for some distance, but withheld the stroke until his agonised shouts of "is it a boar" were answered."

Then on 23rd April comes the sad entry:—

"Steele and Brooke and the Honorary Secretary got away after a pig bright and early; Brooke disappeared and the other two had a real cheery hunt—a ding dong gallop—and a good fight at the end. On returning to line found Brooke much shaken and his horse dying, broken back.

Meeting an old well, absolutely blind, and eight feet deep at the broadest part, the good nag got over 21 feet, dropped his hind quarters in with the inevitable result. A gun shot on the still morning air and the line continued with heavy hearts. York accompanied Brooke (on charpoy); latter badly shaken.

All feel the deepest sympathy with this real good sportsman who "has shunned delights and lived laborious days" in order to buy two good horses, with which he took infinite pains."

It is not surprising that Brooke was "badly shaken" as, though neither he nor they knew it at the time, he had broken his neck, though fortunately it had not been dislocated. His neck grew quite stiff and very much swollen, and he was recommended to have massage, but the masseur hurt him so much that Arthur drove him off.

That all happened on the 23rd April and on the 18th May, Arthur is recorded as having been out again, showing his courage and the tough stuff he was made of. On the 19th the diary states "the right heat killed their pig, Brooke getting the spear" and on the same day later on, they were on to another pig, "all work was done by Brooke who speared." This went on quite regularly till the end of the season. Later, as his neck was still stiff and sore and did not seem to be improving, Arthur took his short leave at home to see a specialist who had him X-rayed, and was enchanted to find that he had a patient who had broken his neck and survived, there not being many recorded cases of this at that time. He told Arthur that it was fortunate for him that he had driven off the masseur, as massage so soon after the accident was the one thing wanted to complete the job. The break never seems to have come against him, though there was an idea that it had affected his sight, but that was not so.

Arthur was always short-sighted and there was some fear when he went up for his medical that he might be spun for that reason. He got his jacket in 1914 and served in the 29th Division in Gallipoli. He was later recommended for a D.S.O. Nothing more was heard of this, but the French gave him the Legion of Honour. From Gallipoli he went to Mesopotamia where he served under Maude in the advance to and capture of Baghdad. He was wounded and three times mentioned in despatches, and was then awarded the D.S.O. The description of the action on 25th February 1916 for which he received this award is given in Edmund Candler's book—"The Long Road to Baghdad."

"Touch with the enemy was temporarily lost but at 11.30 a.m. when the Loyal North Lancashires, who formed the rear guard, came under artillery fire at long range, Capt. Brooke's Battery (66th Brigade R.F.A.) pushed on and came into action three-quarters of a mile ahead of the infantry. This man-oeuvre was brilliantly carried out and diverted the fire from the North Lancashires, who deployed and drove the enemy from his advance posts."

In this action he must have used the contraption which he called "a special observation ladder" of which the following is a description copied out of his diary. In spite of what he says in the diary I have been told that Arthur did go close up to the front in this thing and took not the slightest notice of any attempts to dislodge him:—

"Observation was done from a special observation ladder made by the sappers at Amarah for us. It consisted of three ordinary ladders about eleven feet long. Each ladder was a different width. The widest part went at the bottom and the narrowest part at the top, the pieces fitted together into sockets. A sort of steel shield was fitted on to the top of the top piece, and the whole thing took about twenty minutes to erect and required about twenty men to erect it. It was supported by guy ropes attached to picketing pegs. It gave your eye about thirty feet above the ground, which, in this country which is like a billiard table, gives you a very good view. The shield was bullet proof at point blank range. I have had it up within 800 yards of the Turkish front line but at ranges of 1200 yards you could generally see everything that was going on, in fact during the progress of a fight the staff got nearly all their information from the occupants of the ladders. It was invaluable throughout all the trench warfare, but when the battery moved it did so at night and dug in, and it was easy to carry the ladder up and erect it at night well in advance of the gun position. Later on when it came to moving fighting, it was not quite so useful though much better than none at all. It took too long to put up and if you tried to take it up close to the firing line, a machine gun was turned on at once and you had to get out or get under. It was a clumsy thing to cart about too, especially when you were not overburdened with transport. As a matter of fact I had found a derelict limbered A.S. wagon without a pole and with broken wheels and had rigged this up with my spare gun wheels and a spare pole and it carried the ladder, telephones, cable and some light refreshments, and used to come along with the guns till it was wanted. Some blighter on the Staff of course spotted it, as was bound to happen, and realised that it was an unauthorised vehicle. A signal officer who had lost one of his limbered wagons was sent along with a request that the unauthorised one in my possession should be handed over to him. While he was being regaled with beer or some other intoxicant, the pole and the gun wheels were removed from the wagon and when he was taken out and shown it he of course said it was no use to him whatever and went away. I tried this on three times and managed to keep the wagon till the fighting was over and I went on leave, but I think the trick must have leaked out as my successor pro. tem. tried it out a fourth time and was brought up on the mat and severely reprimanded."

In the Diary he gives the following account of the celebrations at Christmas 1916. "We got our tents up from 'Twin Canals', also two cases of brown sherry which had followed me out from the 9th Corps in Egypt, also some beer and whiskey for the men for Christmas. We had quite a pleasant Christmas, plum pudding from the Ladies of Bombay, Champagne from George Nathaniel Curzon, Brown Sherry from No. 1 and Cherry Brandy from the Ladies of India at Simla."

"Number 1" referred to the place from which the Brown Sherry came i.e. George F. Brooke and Son, 1 Gardiner Row, Dublin—the Family Firm. Arthur was always fond of brown sherry and I used to send him two cases at a time at fixed intervals.

He had it all through Gallipoli and always said that as a result, while his officers might have been wounded, not one of them ever went sick. He had a ranker officer who was a tee-totaller. He drank the brown sherry out of a tin mug and said it was very good port.

When peace came he returned to India and then came
back to England as Chief Instructor at Weedon. He went
back to India again but was retired in 1936 as a Major (though
he had been a Brevet Lieutenant Colonel for years). He had
fallen foul of his immediate superiors, each time fighting the
battle of someone else who in his opinion was being unjustly
treated; the first time it was a subaltern at Aldershot, and the
second time a farrier sergeant in India.

In January 1922 a cousin of my Father's, Mrs. Dermot
Doyne[1] sent him a letter which she had received from an
ex-soldier in Carlow.

> Hacketstown,
> Co. Carlow.
> Jan. 27 1922.

Dear Madam,

    I am writing in reference to my service in the late
war. I have been out East with Major Brooks D.S.O.,
for a period of three years and two months in Mesopotamia and we fought side by side from Omara to
the frontier of Russia which covers hundreds of miles.
We had the pleasure of capturing Baghdad. We made
the Turks surrender and hand in there guns and
ammunition and released our British prisoners under
the command of Major Brooks D.S.O. We were then
called to rest we rested two days 75 of his men were
picked myself among the number. We were posted
to S. Battery of the royal horse Artillery. We fought
for twenty-one days and nights four of them without
food or water at the captureing of Cutlamaara which
there was a sight we shall never forget the Golden
Temple. We had ninty horses starting twenty
coming back. We were still under the command of
Major Brooks and Colonel Castle of the Lancers.

---

[1]Daughter of Rt. Hon. Frank Brooke, P.C.

ARTHUR; 1886–1954

I there had the pleasure of seeing the Major seated on
Horseback giving the word of Command to his troops
wounded. But still kept his seat the Blood flowing
from his wound and rolled into his boots his men
were proud of him also he was proud of his men
he was a brave and gallant soldier. It was a severe
battle before we captured it. We blew up the Railway Station and seventeen of there trains next
day they surrendered and we rushed hard to have the
honour of the Temple when the battle was over we
were called to rest the Major treated us like gentlemen. He sent his wagons back 50 miles for good
whiskey and ciggarettes for us. When we joined the
66th Brigade D. battery our comrades called us
scare crows. It was small blame for them. We told
them we were the fighting soldiers not like them
behind the line. Dear Madam after all our fighting
for King and Country They treated me very badly
for the Hardships I endured I have been in Hospital
for six months with Dysentery and Rheumatic pains
I havent been treated very fairly I had joined the
Depot at Jubellapore for three weeks when I was
picked for frontier of India when I got there I was
medically unfit and had garrison at Lahore. The
soldiers that never seen the front were better treated
than I was They gave me no pension only my
Gratuity and I am a Mons hero at that. Dear
Madam I wish to ask you a favour to send me
Major Brooks address as I wish to write to him I
called at Tullow House but I was informed you were
at Coolattin Park. The Major told me Mrs. Doyne
of Tullow was his first cousin.

Yours respectfully
D 66BG L Brennan 12624 RFA

153

The spelling is Gunner Brennan's. The general account is fairly accurate except for the number of horses and their losses. "Colonel Castle" is Colonel Cassel and "Cutlamara" is Samarra, the furthest point they reached beyond Baghdad. "Omara" might be Amara—but in fact they started from Busrah. For some reason the letter never was sent to Arthur in India. My father dealt with it in the way that Gunner Brennan hoped and Arthur would have wished, and then probably forgot all about it and lost the original. Fortunately I had kept a copy. I showed the copy to Arthur years afterwards and he remembered Gunner Brennan quite well.

When he was Chief Instructor at Weedon, Arthur had a rather notorious Baby Austin. Either it (or someone else's Morris Minor) held the record for the trip from Weedon to the War Office, lost time being made up through the traffic in London. He once drove me, late for dinner, from St. John's Wood to the Rag. It was a hair-raising performance and I commented on how unmoved his servant, a very tall man, had been all through it—sitting in the back.

Arthur said grimly "He's a man of iron nerve." Once they had a smash at a cross-roads on the way to a meet—the servant sitting coiled up in the back as usual. When they were taken out, Arthur asked the servant if he was hurt, and hearing that all was well, said "Well isn't that damned unfair, and look at me." They went on to the nearest hospital where Arthur demanded to be patched up so that he might continue on his way and have his day's hunting. He was much surprised and rather indignant, when the surgeon cleaned him up, put some stitches in him, gave him various injections and put him to bed.

Arthur was bad enough for the hospital authorities to wire Emily (who got the message at Paddington just as she was starting to Limerick for the hunting) and she had to leave the train and let the rest of the party go on without her.

In November 1928 the 'Morning Post' under the heading

"Mixed Mounts" gave an account of a day's hunting had by Arthur;

"A Lady well known with Midland packs recently lent a friend, a soldier and a stranger to the county, a horse. Hounds ran well, and shortly he with another well-mounted man found themselves at a railway with hounds checked spread out over the line. Both jumped off their horses and climbed on to the railway with a view to preventing hounds being run over. After the danger had passed they remounted and followed on with the hunt.

In the evening on his return home, the hostess's groom pointed out to the guest that the horse he was on was not that on which he started out. He was totally unaware of this important fact. Search by means of the telephone for long failed to reveal where the right horse was. It was finally ascertained that another soldier, well known in sporting circles for his prowess as a rider, had got the horse, and equally had been unaware of the change until his groom pointed it out on his return. He was heard to remark that he had noticed the horse's mouth had improved, but put it down to alteration in the curb chain. Both horses were chestnuts."

While he was at Weedon, Arthur and I went for a trip in France in the Baby Austin. When we were arranging details I mentioned to him that he would have to put up his Legion of Honour.

He said, "Don't be stupid, you can't do a thing like that. You don't suppose that I am going to drive through France with a cross hanging on my coat."

I explained that that was unnecessary—(of course he knew this already). All he had to do was to put a small scarlet ribbon in his button hole. Arthur said he did not know where he could get such a thing, so I said "You leave it to me", and fixed it in his buttonhole the moment we landed at Calais. It bore fruit, as when we were having dinner "Au Grand Cerf" at Les Andelys, the Proprietor came up and said "Je vois que Monsieur est decoré". He himself had the Croix de Guerre. Finally it turned out that he also was a gunner and that his battery had been not very far from Arthur's in Gallipoli. He said we must have a drink on the House. The choice was put up to me and I suggested Calvados. He was very pleased as he had some which was very old and made by his family. They made fresh supplies every year and kept some back to get really old; this old stuff was only produced on special occasions "like the present". It was first class. You could get the flavour of the apple and the flavour of the brandy. It was smooth and went down like new milk.

We went to Rouen and Chartres, a short trip through the Château country, and back through Burgundy, Rheims, and Epernay to Calais.

One morning I said to Arthur that it was curious that so far we had not met any one-way streets. He became very British, and said you would not expect to find them in a country like this. A quarter of an hour later we were in Tours and he said

"What's Sens Unique?"

I said "It's one-way traffic and judging by the uproar, you're going through it the wrong way."

"Oh! Well! there's nothing to do but tread on the gas."

This he proceeded to do, and we tore up the street amid shouts and blowing of whistles but got through without any incident, and what was more wonderful still, never heard anything more about it.

Next we met two children away in the country leading a dog that had a resemblance to a fox hound. Arthur ordered me to find out if there was a pack of hounds in the neighbourhood. He could talk just as much or as little French as I could, but always flatly refused to try it out and left all the talking to me. I questioned the children, and their first reply was that the dog's name was César. I tried again, and they said that there were hounds at the Château de Cheverny, close by. We went off there, found the kennels and an old lady came to tell us all about them.

Arthur said,

"Tell her we want to talk to the huntsman."

"What's huntsman, in French?"

"Try piqueur."

So I asked if it was possible to see Monsieur le Piqueur to talk to him about the hounds.

The old lady said quite firmly that that was impossible; he was her husband and she knew that he was digging the potatoes and could not be disturbed. Arthur used a very coarse expression for "nonsense" and told me to get on with it. I said this was a great "dommage, parceque Monsieur ici est grand chasseur en Angleterre."

I learnt afterwards that what I had told her was something to the effect that when in England, Arthur was a tall page boy.

She went off to tell her husband, and I suppose, he, overcome with curiosity to see this phenomenon who wished to talk to him about hounds, came back with her. The old man looked like a coachman of many years back, dressed in a black coat with a flat made-up stock which had a brass horse shoe pin stuck in it. And then the conversation began.

"Ask him where he gets his hounds."

It must be realised that each time I spoke there was quite a delay while I translated Arthur's question to myself.

The hounds came from "Sir Jardine, un Milord ecossais."

"Ask him if they have good noses?"

This completely floored me so I said, "Est ce qu'ils ont bon" and then I gave three terrific snuffles like a child with a cold

157

11

in its nose, and the huntsman was delighted and said, "Le flair? Mais oui, magnifique!"

By this time I was a nervous wreck but Arthur appeared satisfied and did not seem to want any more information, so having tipped the huntsman, we went into the Château, which, as everyone knows, is beautiful.

After he left the army Arthur managed Captain Brassey's stud farm at Orchardstown, near Fethard. While there he had a very bad motor smash (not in the Baby Austin) when a bus came downhill on a bend, completely out of control and on the wrong side of the road, and drove straight into him. Arthur was very badly broken up, and though he recovered at the time, physically he never quite got over the effects of that accident. The jury soothed him by awarding him his costs and £2,250 damages.

When the war came he went back to train the Oxfordshire Yeomanry, but was considered too old to take the Regiment out to France.

For some years Arthur had no fixed abode and stayed about doing a good deal of racing in England. Finally he hung up his hat in my house, coming and going exactly as he wanted, and he was great company for me. He had a horse stabled in the country and hunted in Kildare for three seasons.

He hunted one day a week and sometimes two, all through the first half of the 1953-54 season. On coming home from hunting one particular Saturday in the middle of January, he told me he had made an appointment with the doctor for Monday. I enquired of him what was wrong, and he told me that he had a lump on his side which he had noticed first when in England just before he came over to Ireland for the hunting.

An operation was performed to give him relief but he died in April of that year. Arthur endured all the pain and discomfort without a murmur; he met death with the same lighthearted courage he'd always shown to the troubles and difficulties he had come up against in life.

10. *Salary and Sinecure*

BACK in 1902 when I had left Winchester I started off as
a clerk in an Insurance Company in Dublin's Sackville
Street—as it then was. The pay was certainly not enough to
enable one to get into mischief! One unfortunate young man
whose name was Paddy Power received the generous sum of
£10 per annum. The Company had not the face to hand
over the paltry sum of 3/10d. per week, so at the end of each
month Power was solemnly given a cheque for 16/8d. duly
signed by the Branch Manager and a local Director—who
drew a guinea for his attendance. Compared to Power I
was rich, as I had started on £25 a year and when I left at
the end of five years, by which time Power was dead, I was
getting £45. Probably I was not worth more.

We never knew at what time our working day would end,
as the heads of the office spent most of their day gossiping

in front of the fire in a back room; surfacing at about 3.30 p.m., they rattled through their work, leaving Paddy Power and myself to clear up after they had finished. One day the telephone rang just as we were leaving, and I answered it and was asked who was speaking. With great presence of mind I imitated the caretaker's voice and said, "They're all gone!" The Manager of the Company was generally out most of the day hunting business, at which he was most successful, and he had no idea of the way his seconds-in-command did *their* part.

But if I earned small pay I got good value for myself in other ways. My seat was in the window and I did not miss much that went on in Sackville Street. Sometimes there was a fight among the flower-women at the foot of Nelson's Pillar, those who were not actively engaged seeming always to take the line that it was best to let the combatants fight it out to a finish.

Then Signor Magini, the Dancing Master (whose real name I always suspected was Magennis) used to walk by, a miracle of deportment. He wore an immaculate frock coat, light grey trousers, lavender coloured gloves, a flower in his buttonhole and of course—a tall hat. His moustache was waxed to points, he carried in one hand a magenta coloured silk handkerchief, and in the other a long black cane with a silver knob at the top. On this he leant quite lightly and as the stick and his arm swayed, his body swayed with them in perfect rhythm, and strictly from the hips. On other days he rode past, when his light grey trousers were cut for riding and strapped under his boots, while a smart cutting whip took the place of the stick. His horse from time to time gave the least little caracole and the Signor swayed his body with the movements of the horse in the most graceful manner imaginable.

I could always recognise from a little way off the hoof-beats

160

of the horses in my mother's carriage, and so was ready to wave to her as she went by.

Quite regularly every afternoon Mrs. Dickinson, Parnell's sister, drove by in her phaeton. This was a very smart, if slightly eccentric turnout; the horses were black, whilst all the harness was white, and there was a very smart tiger sitting up behind. Mrs. Dickinson herself always wore a scarlet cape, usually a black toque and of course a veil. She said that on these afternoon drives, she was the "admiration of Dublin[1]!" Her phaeton passed up one side of Sackville Street, turned round at the Rotunda and drove back on the other side.

There were not many incidents in the office itself. On one occasion however when I went up to the Manager with his basket he said to me—"It's very sad about——, isn't it?" I thought it easier to say "Yes", than to say that I did not know who he was talking about and he went on—"I was speaking to him only the night before last"...I said "It must have been very sudden". And he said, "It usually *is* when you commit suicide".

Quite trivial things entertained us during the day. For instance a small boy came in one day with the usual request for a copper to help him to break his fast, as he had not eaten anything for twenty-four hours; I said I would give him sixpence if he'd stand on his head...the lad immediately did so —and coins showered out of his pockets on to the floor.

Another day my immediate boss—Alex. MacGregor, who came from Renfrew—said to me, "Mr. Brooke, your books are like a dog's breakfast". And that was no more than the truth. The calligraphy taught at Laleham and Winchester was not the kind suitable for writing in ancient policy registers—wherein all my predecessors had made the entries in perfect copper-plate.

---

[1] "A Patriot's Mistake". Emily Monroe Dickinson. Dublin, Hodges Figgis & Co. Ltd.

Nevertheless—and in spite of the foregoing—during the years I worked for the Insurance Company, their business in Ireland increased in a most satisfactory fashion.

About half-way through my career in the Insurance office, I came in for a windfall. My mother's cousin, Dunbar Barton, was made Justice of the Chancery Division in Dublin. In addition to a salary of £3,000 per annum, he had the privilege of appointing a train-bearer for himself, at a salary of £100 —and into that office I walked. As a result I had to fit myself out with a court suit of fine black cloth with Limerick lace ruffles at the cuffs, and a jabot of the same at the collar, knee-breeches, silk stockings and shoes with buckles, a court sword and a cocked hat which was not intended to be worn.

In this attire I accompanied Dunbar on the day of the opening of the Easter Term to 12 Merrion Square where the Lord Chancellor (Lord Ashbourne) lived, and where he held his levee before going in procession to the Four Courts. All the judges, including the Lord Chief Justice (Lord O'Brien, the famous Peter the Packer) Chief Baron Christopher Palles, and the Master of the Rolls, Sir Andrew Porter were at the levee. The Lord Chancellor and the Master of the Rolls also had train-bearers, and the Lord Chancellor had his purse-bearer as well, and an attendant who carried the mace. I think the purse was originally intended to hold the Great Seal of Ireland. It was a magnificent affair about fifteen inches by ten, of velvet on which the Royal Arms with Crest and Supporters were heavily embroidered, and it had gold cords and tassels. It was the private property of the Lord Chancellor. Whether he paid for it or not at the beginning, I do not know, but it was certainly his when he ceased to hold office.

I was presented to the Lord Chancellor, then took a place in the background with the other train-bearers and the purse-bearer. I had never met the Lord Chancellor before, but later I got to know him quite well through playing bridge with him in Kildare Street Club. He always spoke in ordinary conversation as if delivering judgement in the Appeal Court of the House of Lords. One night we had played fairly late, and the following morning—sitting next to me at breakfast— he made a rather startling statement when one considers the circumstances of its delivery. "I usually play bridge at the Athenaeum Club. Now at the Athenaeum, there are good players, bad players, and indifferent players, but all very honourable gentlemen". . . I left it at that!

At the levee Dunbar took his place near the Lord Chancellor, and all the judges as they arrived ranged up on either side; then all the Bar came in, and each of them made his bow to the Lord Chancellor. When the levee was over, the judges proceeded in their carriages to the Four Courts headed by the Lord Chancellor with his retinue.

While we drove through the streets from Merrion Square, Dunbar explained to me that all this state was kept by the Lord Chancellor and the judges with the intention of display-ing and upholding the majesty of the Law.

I was much impressed—feeling that at a-hundred-a-year I would be delighted to help them in the good work for as long as they liked.

On arrival at the Four Courts a procession was formed under the Dome. The Mace-bearer headed it, followed by the purse-bearer, and then came the Lord Chancellor, his train held up by the bearer. The judges followed in order, including Dunbar, his train upheld by me. Then the judges went into some room for a meeting of the Benchers, and we train-bearers etc., retired to a room reserved for us. I was much younger than any of the others and the Lord Chancellor's purse-bearer, who had been longer at the job than anyone else, told us anecdotes of past Lord Chancellors and their train-bearers. The only one that remains in my recollection concerns a one-time purse-bearer who had evidently been a little odd. He always put a sixpenny piece into the purse, in case the Lord Chancellor might be moved to distribute largesse on his arrival at the Four Courts.

This was the only occasion on which I attended Dunbar as he always said that he was afraid I might trip and pull him over backwards. He did not seem to realise that his life was far too valuable for me to do anything so careless. My outgoings that day were ten shillings—five for cab hire and five for Dunbar's crier who fetched the cab—so that as I drew the salary for ten years my fee for that day's work came to £999. 10. 0. less income tax, which was not very high in those days (although Mr. Asquith—I think it was—*did* say that it was too high for peacetime), and of course I had the earned income allowance. In addition to the salary, as the holder of an office in the Law Courts, I was exempt from all jury service. The knowledge that I am among the few people left who has held a real sinecure fills me with pleasure. One result of being the possessor of a court suit was that I was now able to go to the Lord Lieutenant's levee and so was invited to balls at the Castle. I got to know many people who were giving parties and dances and had quite a gay time. Another result was that in course of time I was in a position to buy two Guinness Ordinary £10 shares at £56 each, by which means I acquired merit with my father who was always urging me to save money—without explaining how it could be done on £25 a year. And then I bought a motor bicycle. It was the one-hundred-and-ninety-third motor vehicle of any kind to be registered in County Dublin. There were no petrol pumps in those days and if you went to the country it was advisable to have a two-gallon tin of petrol strapped on to the back of the bicycle. This two-gallon tin cost 2/8d. and you got two shillings back when you returned the empty tin.

Once I was prosecuted in the police court in Green Street and fined ten shillings for riding this bicycle at twenty-six miles an hour up the main road of the Phoenix Park, which is a straight two miles and about one hundred and twenty feet wide. Wall, K.C., the Divisional Magistrate, who heard the case, had a long discussion with the prosecuting Sergeant Kenoy 22D, as to whether the Act covered four-wheeled vehicles only in which case my bicycle could not be included. In the course of this argument the Magistrate referred to my bicycle as "one of these puffing billies", which I thought rather rude, but as the remark produced "laughter in Court" he and everyone else was satisfied. Finally he asked me if I would be satisfied to be dealt with on the spot and as I had views of Sergeant Kenoy 22D and myself ending up in the House of Lords (I paying costs all the way) I was graciously pleased to be fined 10/–.

My greater freedom in the way of transport and my greater social efforts led me to be asked about to lunch and dinner, and one house that I frequently went to on Sundays was that of John Hatchell (who will be remembered as sharing the carriage with Mrs. B. at Geneva) at Fortfield, Terenure. He lived there with his nieces who were great friends and contemporaries of my mother. They were very kind in asking me and Sunday lunches there were always interesting. They were usually centred about some distinguished guest and there was little necessity for me to try to make conversation. It was best to listen. One Sunday the "guest" was Dr. Mahaffy[1] and no one of any calibre was asked to meet him, for leaving him to hold the field undisturbed was the best way of getting him to talk. On this occasion he ranged over the Middle West of America, and then having given us a quite wonderful talk on Ancient Greece, wound up with Egypt. Some famous Egyptologist had just written a new book on the subject of the "Book of the Dead" and Mahaffy talked on this for some time. Then suddenly he turned to me and said, "That is a subject you ought to know something about and you should get this book and study it".

---

[1]John Pentland Mahaffy, Provost of Trinity College.

The following day I added half an hour to my lunchtime and went to the best bookshop in Dublin where I told an elderly gentleman with whiskers, and dressed rather formally in a black morning coat, that I wanted to buy a copy of this particular book. He only said—"You could not afford that book, and if you could, you would not understand it". Feeling that he was probably quite correct in both his statements I went out of the shop.

Another interesting party to which I was asked at a much later date was the Christmas Lunch at Guinness's Brewery. (Let no one on any account ever refuse an invitation to that Lunch). There was a hot ham, the like of which I never saw anywhere else. I almost wept at the thought that it was going to be cut, but a Brewer had other ideas. He took up a carving knife and before anyone could stop him, made a huge gash in the ham—at the wrong end! The Head Waiter and the Caterer almost passed out but a Managing Director said quietly, and with perfect manners, "Oh! . . . thank you very much, but don't bother, the Head Waiter will carve the ham for us".

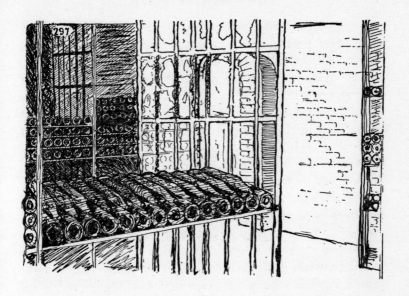

11. *Portraits and Port*

ON Christmas Eve 1906, the confidential clerk in my
father's business died of pneumonia after a short illness.
On the following day my father told me that he proposed
taking me into the family business, as soon as I could make the
necessary arrangements with the Insurance Company. Then,
on New Year's Day, my father's Manager committed suicide,
and I found myself pitchforked into George Brooke and Son
—the Governor's business—at a moment's notice, to take
charge.

I did not know the first thing about wine, and extremely little
about running a commercial business—that not being much in
the line of a junior Insurance clerk. However I worked away
at the wine end and never being shy of asking for advice, I
gradually acquired the necessary knowledge. On retiring, forty-
eight years later, I was accounted—and I think rightly so—

167

a good judge of wine, particularly of young wine wanted for buying and putting away to mature for future consumption and to improve in bottle. One thing I realised then, was, that the more I learned the more there was to learn, and that has been true right up to the time I quitted the wine business.

It always amuses me to read newspaper articles written by journalists who have rushed around the Bordeaux vineyards at the end of July (one is tempted to think, in charge of a taxi-driver) wherein the writer firmly states that the coming vintage will be the "vintage of the century", though every sensible man knows that it is quite impossible to make such a statement with any degree of accuracy for many months to come . . . and even then it is unwise to do so.

When in 1921 we wound up the firm of George Brooke & Son at Gardiner Row, in the clearing up there came to light quite a number of bottles, small remnants of bins of very good old clarets, of vintages such as 1858, 1864, 1865, 1870 and 1878. (The 1875's had of course been sold long before). Of the first three, only a small number of the bottles proved to be any good, but it was different with the other two and we had some excellent drinking. The 1870's were then 51 years old, but were delicious. Nearly twenty years later when this wine was approaching seventy years old, a friend of mine, a Shipper's Agent, asked me to dine and drink a bottle of Château Margaux 1870. The wine was reverently decanted by my host as we sat down to dinner and our first glasses were really magnificent. We took some time over them, talking about the wine and enjoying it, and then we had second glasses—only to find that a dreadful thing had happened. The rest of the wine had died in the decanter while we were looking at it and was now quite undrinkable. Let this be a warning never to delay too long discussing the first glass of a very old bottle of claret. If we had followed the text book and decanted the wine a little time before dinner so that it might have taken up the temperature of the room, the probability is that the whole bottle would have been undrinkable.

When I had finished winding-up George Brooke & Son, I went to Thompson D'Olier & Co. in Eustace Street, Dublin. It was the same type of business as ours had been and they had been trading in Eustace Street certainly since before 1798. The Thompsons were the original owners, but finding themselves in difficult straits at the time of the Irish Famine in 1849, they took in Mr. Edmund D'Olier who brought fresh capital. The D'Oliers were Huguenots who came from Montauban in France, having left that country at the time of the Revocation of the Edict of Nantes. They went to Amsterdam where they spent a generation, then came to Dublin where they traded as bankers, bullion brokers, and silversmiths. A small piece of 18th century silver with the mark of Isaac D'Olier fetched £300 at auction in Dublin quite recently. Jeremiah D'Olier, Edmund's father, was among the most important of those who founded the Bank of Ireland in 1782, and D'Olier Street in Dublin was named after him in acknowledgement of his work as one of the Wide Street Commissioners.

Edmund D'Olier, the second, owned the business when I joined in 1921 and when he died in 1935 it was turned into a private limited liability company and I was made Managing Director. I held this appointment until June 1955, when, having been more than forty-eight years a wine merchant and five years an Insurance Clerk, I decided I had done enough—so I retired.

*　　*　　*　　*

In about 1927, whilst still with Thompson D'Olier & Co., I had my one and only excursion into picture dealing and with some success.

When Rochestown, my Barton grandfather's home in Tipperary, was sold the owner, who was Mrs. B.'s nephew, asked her to house the pictures for him. Among them was a conversation piece by Zoffany, a portrait of James Farrell Phipps. Phipps was an Oxford friend of my great-great-grandfather, the Rev. Samuel Riall, whose daughter brought Rochestown into the Barton family on her marriage to my great-grandfather, Dunbar Barton. Phipps, as is shown by letters still in existence, had given the picture to Riall and it had always hung at Rochestown. Phipps was for a long time Member of Parliament for Peterborough and had been one of the party that went with Sir Joseph Banks, P.R.S. on his expedition to Newfoundland in H.M.S. Niger in 1764.

When Mrs. B. died, the owner sold the pictures and the Zoffany was bought by her son, Sir Hugh McCalmont; Major Dermot McCalmont, son of Sir Hugh, now has the picture at Mount Juliet in County Kilkenny, and it has been sent more than once on loan to exhibitions in London.

In about 1927 I was walking up Liffey Street in Dublin—which in the old days was the Street of the Antique Dealers. In the window of Henry Naylor's shop I was astonished to see a picture of Phipps, identical with the Rochestown original which I knew to be at Mount Juliet, while the documents proving its authenticity were actually in my possession. I went into Naylor's and bought the picture for nine pounds. I then wrote to Aunt Rose and Arthur and asked them to come in with me, and the three of us formed a syndicate with equal shares. I set about hunting up the history of the picture and found that it had been bought in a sale at Bennett's auction rooms in Dublin. I was told that it had been put up by Mr. Richard Burke, a well-known collector, who had been Master of the Tipperary Hounds for years, and who by a coincidence, during that time had rented Grove (near Fethard in Tipperary) —the other Barton place. I wrote to Burke asking him about it and though he obviously knew, he refused to tell me anything about the picture, and referred me to Sinclair, a well-known Dublin dealer in pictures and silver. Sinclair was equally

170

mysterious and professed to know nothing about the origin of the picture, so I said . . . "It is by Zoffany". Sinclair said "No! I thought that myself when I first saw it, but it is not by the Master".

I sent the picture over to Aunt Rose's flat in London where it hung for some time. At the time she had some pictures that had belonged to my father, and which she and I had the selling of as trustees of his will. One day someone from the Tate came to look at two Orpens. When he came in he looked around the room and immediately said, "I see you have a Zoffany".

We had had some necessary repairs done to the picture and thought of having it cleaned. The man who did the repairs and to whom we talked about the cleaning was not told who we thought was the painter, but the moment he saw it he said . . . "It's by Zoffany". Aunt Rose asked him how he knew and he said that he had just finished cleaning a large number of Zoffanys belonging to some collection so that he should know what a Zoffany looked like. We told him the story and the next thing we knew was that he sent a short paragraph to a daily paper stating that he was repairing a picture by Zoffany of James Phipps, a replica of the one owned by Major Dermot McCalmont, the well-known breeder and racehorse owner, at Mount Juliet in Ireland.

With that, Zoffany and Phipps climbed on to the band-wagon with "The Tetrarch".

It now seemed certain that the picture was by Zoffany and just about then I for a moment began to regret having partners. I would have liked to keep the picture, but the others were adamant about it and we put it up for sale at Sotheby's. It fetched £200, being bought, we were told, by Dr. Tancred Borenius. I then went back to Sinclair and told him all about the sale and who had bought the picture. He nearly went out through the roof, threw his hands up to Heaven and shouted, "That shows you should always stick to your first instinct

171

and never allow your own better judgement to be over-ruled".

I never told him that I had known all along who was the subject of the portrait, what his history was, or that I knew where the original portrait was. I formed the opinion from all this, that if you know the name and dates of the subject of a portrait of this kind, you are well on the way to finding out who the artist was.

I was still puzzling about where the picture had come from, when one Sunday in Innislonagh Church, near Clonmel, I saw a large monument to Colonel Pownall Phipps of the Honourable East India Company's Service, and I was told that a family of that name had lived for a long time at Oaklands in the neighbourhood. The Colonel was a nephew of James Phipps and it is possible that his father was given a replica of the picture, painted also by Zoffany; how it got into the hands of Burke remains a mystery.

12. *Gentlemen All*

IN January 1907 I was elected to Kildare Street Club. I thought at the time ... and I still think ... that it was a red-letter day for me.

Kildare Street Club is one of the older clubs. It was founded in 1782, but its roots go back much farther than that. Some time about 1760, Patrick Daly had opened a Chocolate House (afterwards called Daly's Coffee House) at 2 Dame Street. At that house in November 1782, the Rt. Honourable William Burton Conyngham, Teller of the Exchequer in Ireland, was black-balled for Daly's Coffee House. There is nothing known as to why he was black-balled; in fact even this piece of history would have been lost if Gilbert when writing his "History of Dublin" had not been given early access to the records of Kildare Street Club. Burton Conyngham and his friends joined in starting a new club and bought a house in Kildare Street which was the home of Kildare Street Club until the early hours of Sunday 11th November 1860. On that morning the house with all the records of the Club was destroyed by fire. Some of the household staff were sleeping in the house, and three of them were burnt to death.

Only the billiard room at the back of the house remained intact. Pictures, valuable furniture, and a library said to be of 15,000 volumes, were all destroyed. There was a complete dinner service of silver, yet so little molten silver was recovered from the ruins that it was thought the dinner service had been stolen and that the thieves had set fire to the house in order to cover their tracks.

The first entry in the first Minute Book now in existence runs:—

"On Sunday 11th November 1860 a destructive fire broke out in the Club House, Kildare Street, when in little more than an hour and a half the whole house was reduced to ashes, and three of the inmates viz. Miss Smith, Housekeeper, Miss Dickson, Barmaid, and Teresa McEvoy, Housemaid, perished in the conflagration. All the records and books of account belonging to the Club from its foundation were lost. The other inmates of the house were miraculously saved by the intrepidity and coolness of Mr. Hughes, Mrs. Mullins and Teresa McNally, thro' the centre windows of the house".

Hughes, Mrs. Mullins and Teresa McNally were completely cut off in the burning building. Teresa McNally was the head kitchenmaid, and she gave the alarm, and told Hughes that the house was on fire. Mrs. Mullins was in Hughes's room, but a veil was drawn over this, the romance not being officially recognised. Teresa McNally got out on to a window sill overlooking Kildare Street, and Hughes, holding the corner of a sheet in his mouth got out beside her. The account given at the inquest is difficult to follow, but what it says is, that Hughes stood on the girl's shoulders, then on her head and she raised him to the roof. He then caught hold of her hands and dragged her up beside him. Then they let down the sheet to Mrs. Mullins who had been left behind, and between them all she was pulled up on to the roof as well. They found seven other women on the roof, and Hughes succeeded in getting the whole party into a house two doors up the street. A public subscription was opened for him.

The next entry in the book records that the Committee had hired No. 5, Leinster Street as temporary premises, and the third that six dozen of sherry had been ordered to be sent in immediately by Mr. Brooke (the Governor) and a further six dozen by Mr. Brennen.

The building that had been destroyed had already been sold to the College of Physicians, and the Club moved into the house it still occupies (which was being built at the time of the fire) in 1861.

The members were a very sociable body and it was understood that when you sat in the Coffee Room, you were expected to talk to whoever was on either side of you, whether or not you knew him—unless he had someone sitting opposite with whom he was obviously engaged in conversation. By this means, a new member, if he was any good, soon got to know and be known by a great many of those who had been in the Club before him. There was always a great gathering for meals and it was quite usual to have to wait for a place; for this reason the total number of guests in the room at one time was limited to six, and no member was allowed to entertain more than two guests at a time, either for lunch or dinner.

Guests had to be domiciled more than fifteen miles from Dublin, it being considered that any man eligible to be invited to a meal in the Club, who lived so close, should come up for election as a member. There was a clock over the service door in the middle of the room facing the windows, and it was a rule that no member might take a guest to sit at any table beyond the clock. This dated from the time when Landlords were suffering from the "no rent" campaign and were being boycotted and shot at; they wished to have a recognised part of the Coffee Room where they could lunch and dine with each other, and discuss their problems, knowing that there was no fear of eavesdropping on the part of an unsuitable guest thoughtlessly brought in by a fellow member. In fact most of the rooms in the Club were hedged about with restrictions as regarded guests, and if you brought anyone in who had not either lunched or dined in the Club, you might only take him into a room, admittedly very comfortable, known as the "Stranger's Room".

Like all respectable Clubs, Kildare Street Club had its characters, long before, and even up to my time, and after. Lord Clonmell (Earlie) used to stay with Lord Drogheda at Moore Abbey for shoots, and he complained that as nothing but turf or wood was burnt in that house, it was very cold. He arrived, on one occasion, with a good deal of luggage, and whilst he was being welcomed in the Hall, a footman went staggering upstairs with a portmanteau—which suddenly burst open and covered the whole place with coal. It was also said that at a garden party at Buckingham Palace, an old lady smiled charmingly at Lord Clonmell as she was wheeled past in a bath-chair. He rushed up to her and the astonished Queen Victoria found her hand being warmly wrung by Lord Clonmell, who at the same time was saying . . . "I *do* apologise, Madam. I know your face quite well, but I simply cannot remember your name".

The first day I lunched in the Club after election, I saw a very neatly trimmed old man being pushed into the room in a wheelchair. I asked my neighbour who he was, and he said, "That's old Bond-Shelton. He's one of the last survivors of the 'Birkenhead'. He has lost the use of his legs; a shark made at him and bit him, but found him so sour that he spat him out".

Bond-Shelton always went to the Riviera for the early Spring, and some weeks after I first saw him it was reported that the hotel in which he was staying had caught fire, and that he had been rescued through the window of his room by the firemen, and that they had brought out two French ladies from the room with him.

Another character, but before my time, was Captain Sandes —known among the waiters as the "White Tiger". He suffered from fits—a peculiarity of which was, that if he came to from one of them, and found someone trying to help him, he attacked the Good Samaritan in a most savage manner. The result was, that when in one of these fits he fell into the firegrate, beyond seeing that he was not going to burn to death, no one went to his assistance, and when he came to and stood up, a piece of hot coal on which he had been lying was still stuck to the side of his head.

There was another member—James Harrison—who on one occasion got up to kick the fire into a blaze. It was during the war when there was very little fuel, and he had been using the poker to such an extent that it had been necessary to remove the fire-irons altogether. He was very fat, and all of a sudden he overbalanced, fell to the floor and lay there on his back groaning and calling for help. Unfortunately for him the only person nearby was a member with whom Harrison was not on speaking terms. On being asked what he had done by way of help, this member replied—"James was far too heavy for me to try to shift him, so I just shouted at him— 'Get up, you bloody idiot!' and he did".

Horse Show Week was the high spot of the year. Every bedroom in the Club was filled, and the Coffee Room was packed every day for lunch and dinner.

One year (sometime in the eighteen-eighties) it was decided after dinner one evening, that there should be a race from the steps of the Club up to the Shelbourne Hotel corner in St. Stephen's Green, and back. To keep the course, hack-cabs were engaged and they stood head-to-tail across the street at each end and where Molesworth Street comes into Kildare Street. It was a very still night and those who did not run in the race lined the street, some of them holding the silver candle-sticks from the Coffee Room tables.

The race was won by John Watson, the famous Master of the Meath Hounds, but Mr. Henry Persse (Atty's father, and a much older man than John Watson) who came in second, always declared that John did not run the course, but hid in the shadow of the gates of Leinster House, and joined in on the return journey when the others were all tired. You could do things in Dublin in those days! That was long before the time when the jarveys declared that "the polis" were the greatest annoyance they had, and kept a flap of the rug hanging down at the back of the car so as to hide the number.

The cabs which kept the course were stationed on the cab and car rank in Nassau Street, opposite the bow window of the Morning Room of the Club. There was quite a number of these cabs whose owners were largely dependent on the members of the Club for their livelihood. Most of these men had good horses, particularly the ones they drove in their cars and at all times among them there were some first-class Whips. The most famous was Tallon, of whom one of his admirers (who himself owned cars on the rank) said that when he took the reins in his hands to start out on a drive, "Ye'd think they were on fire".

A man called Saul succeeded to most of his business, but as a Whip, while he aped Tallon, he was not in the same category, nor were his horses or vehicles. Probably he was a better business man than Tallon, as he had more men in his employment and more cabs, cars, and horses. He sent a cab once to Summerton to drive Mrs. B. and her sister Mrs. Barklie, and their two daughters. Whatever happened, soon after they left the door at a fairly rapid trot the cab overbalanced on the camber of the avenue and there was a dreadful smash. Two of the occupants were unconscious and badly concussed and the other two were cut by broken glass. Someone said to Saul, "That was a very bad job you did at Summerton. What happened?" Saul said, "I'll tell you, Sir, in one word. The horse was blind, the way was steep, the ladies of course had the cab overloaded, and the driver was totally *inadequate* to the job".

The original hackney-cabs in Dublin were quite high off the ground; the wheels and all the undercarriage were painted lemon yellow, the lower half of the cab itself was a deep rose and the upper half was black. These colours must have had some significance and they may have derived from the hackney carriages of the early 18th century. Until the turn of the century there were no such things as rubber tyres, and with the ill-fitting windows and the rattle of the tyres on the cobblestones, the noise inside the cab was almost deafening. Later on, the cabs were almost always dark-green, that being probably a more practical colour, but the old rose and black cabs with the yellow undercarriage gave a very pleasant dash of colour to the streets. All of these cabs and cars were built by a firm called Sanderson in Dominick Street, Dublin, and it is probable that for more than a century they were responsible for all the vehicles that plied for hire in Dublin. With the arrival of the motor, the hack-cars and cabs disappeared from the scene and with them a very attractive body of men with their gay cabs, outside cars and good horses. They were amusing men, good conversationalists, and if you were on an outside car they were excellent company on a long drive.

*   *   *   *

Among the Lodges on the roll of the Grand Lodge of Freemasons of Ireland, there is the Meridian No. XII.

This Lodge is composed entirely of members of Kildare Street Club. I was initiated in it in 1909 and have spent many happy years in the Lodge. In 1930 the Grand Master, Lord Donoughmore, appointed me his Deputy Grand Master, and he re-appointed me each year until he resigned. Just before his death he recommended me to Grand Lodge as being suitable to succeed him. The Grand Lodge adopted his suggestion and I was installed Grand Master in December 1948 and have been re-elected each year since then.

I have had many interesting experiences which might never have come my way save for my position in the Masonic Order in Ireland. When the present Grand Master of the United Grand Lodge of England—the Earl of Scarbrough— was installed at a Special Convocation in the Albert Hall, the privilege fell to me (as Grand Master of the oldest Grand Lodge in the world, after the Grand Lodge of England) of making the first speech of congratulation.

I have three times had the honour of dining with the Lord Mayor of London at the Mansion House and of lunching with him once.

In this connection I once hailed a taxi in Pall Mall and told the driver to take me to the Mansion House. He looked at me and said, "Wot?" I admit that my overcoat had seen better days but it was the best I had, so I repeated—"The Mansion House", and got into the taxi. Nearing the place he opened his little window and asked, "D'yer mean the Toob Station?" I had had enough of this, and I roared at him, "No! I mean the Mansion House where the Lord Mayor of London lives, and drive me up to the side entrance, that's the one I usually go in by".

Yes! my years in Meridian No. XII and Kildare Street Club have indeed been pleasant, worthwhile ones; they have also been years that have seen extraordinary changes in world affairs—truly spanning a period of 'history in the making'.

But as one grows old, the things that increase infinitely in value—the things that become most precious—are friendship and congenial company, and these I have had, and still possess, in full measure. On this note I shall close my book of memories, and allow the 'brimming river' to take me where it will . . . .

Gloria Finis

Appendix A

IT is not known for certain from what immediate branch of the Brooke family in England Sir Basil Brooke came. The English parentage of the Elizabethan adventurers to Ireland is notoriously difficult to pinpoint.

It is almost certain however that Sir Basil Brooke's father was Oliver Brooke of Warwick whose Grandfather was Rafe Broke of Nantwich. Rafe was second son of Thomas Broke of Leighton, Cheshire, and brother of Sir Richard Broke, Chief Baron of the Exchequer to Henry VIII. Rafe Broke is described as Governor of Calais in Harleian MSS. 1535, folio 92. In the funeral entry of Sir Basil Brooke in the Genealogical Office in Dublin Castle, his Arms are shown as Brooke of Leighton with a crescent for difference which were the Arms of Broke of Nantwich.

(Information supplied by Basil G. Brooke).

Appendix B

BROOKE'S HARRIERS

MY father started his first pack of Harriers in the year 1869 but in a short time there was an outbreak of rabies and this pack had to be destroyed. He started again and bred a second pack to his own ideas, to be dwarf foxhounds from the best blood in England and suitable for hunting hares. He based the breeding of his hounds on Belvoir and Brocklesby blood and was a firm believer in white, black and tan. This pack of my father's was one of the first, *if not the very first,* pack of dwarf foxhounds bred for hunting hares. He seems to have started with harriers and in his early days bought small bitches from the Belvoir draft and thus gradually bred the type of hound which he had set as his aim from the beginning. As time went on he kept up the pack by using as stallion hounds, outside those of his own breeding, dog hounds that he could find on the small side of Belvoir and Brocklesby blood.

In the list for 1904-5 the oldest dog hound is Vanguard, (bred by my father) by Belvoir Vaulter out of his own Heedful.

The next mention of a stallion hound not of his own breeding is Meath Render, the sire of Riot and Victress.

Render's breeding was:—

	Sire	Dam
Meath Render	Rajah	Woodbine
Woodbine	Grove Scrooby	Meath Wisdom
Wisdom	Brocklesby Warlike	Their Niobe
Rajah	Lord Fitzwilliam's Richmond	Durable
Durable	Brocklesby Drummer	Their Gratitude
Richmond	Milton Romulus	Lord Fitzwilliam's Streamlet
Streamlet	Milton Stormer	Their Niobe.

There are five second season and five first season hounds all by Colonel Robertson's Rutland. Rutland's breeding was by Mr. Craig's Tapster out of Holm Hill Rosie by Belvoir Gambler.

My father never showed his hounds at Peterborough, but both Colonel Robertson-Aikman and Mrs. Cheape (The Squire) who *did* show with great success, often used his stallion hounds.

"Brooke's Harriers", as they were called (B.H. was on the button) hunted all around Leixlip and Lucan and away to the foothills of the Dublin Mountains beyond Tallaght and Brittas. The pack was very popular with the farmers; the field was always small so they did no damage and this hunting gave the farmers a good opportunity to bring out their young horses and give them their first sight of hounds. My father hunted the pack entirely at his own expense, and the farmers supported him worthily by the generous way they provided first-class walks for his puppies. In 1895 about twenty-five years after he had founded the pack, these farmers and other friends joined to make him a presentation of some splendid plate. Then in 1906 for the sake of economy, the pack was given up. Many of the hounds were bought by Captain Hardy who hunted around the neighbourhood of Maynooth, calling the pack, the Grangewilliam Harriers. After a few years he gave up and the hunt was kept going by subscription and was known as the North Kildare Harriers, but there was a sad lack of that knowledge of the breeding of hounds required to keep up anything like the old standard. Some years after the 1914–18 war my brother Francis took over the North Kildare Harriers, finding among them a few bitches left of the old blood, from which he started to restore the pack. He had inherited my father's wonderful flair for breeding hounds, and at Peterborough in 1927 won with Vaulter, the Champion Cup for single dog hounds not less than their second season and not over 21 inches, and the

Champion Cup for single bitches with Spiteful. Unfortunately my father had died the year before this event which would have given him so much pleasure. Francis gave up the North Kildare Harriers when he became Joint Master of the Kildare Hounds.

My father's kennels were built under his supervision by a local mason, James Neill. The general plan, with certain alterations to suit his own needs, was worked out by him from the suggestions for kennels in Peter Beckford's "Thoughts on Hunting".